Praise

Jes

Our Refuge

"In *Jesus Our Refuge*, Matt invites us to discover new depths in our relationship with Jesus. Matt's writing style is clever and engaging, rich in wisdom, and filled with fresh insights on every page. I highly recommend this book. In every chapter, you will grow deeper in love with Jesus and be amazed by His love for you."

—Dr. Bob Schuchts
John Paul II Healing Center

"Matt has given us a remarkable gift, for he exposes critical aspects of our spiritual struggle too often overlooked or unseen. He then masterfully reveals Jesus as the definitive answer to these needs, our awesome Saviour and desperately needed refuge. This book is a wake-up call, a bracing and honest evaluation of our authentic spiritual needs, and an invitation to enter God's loving plan more deeply than ever before."

—Bishop Scott McCaig C.C.
Military Ordinary of Canada

Jesus
Our Refuge

Jesus
Our Refuge

Matt Fradd

**SPIRIT OF WISDOM
PRESS**

ISBN: 978-1-968630-02-7

Printed in the United States of America   0 9 1 1 2 5

♾This paper meets the requirements of ANSI/NISO Z39.48-1992 (Permanence of Paper)

To

John Eldredge

Blessed are all who take refuge in Him.

Psalm 2:12

Contents

Introduction

Come to me, all you who are weary
and burdened, and I will give you rest.
Matthew 11:28

These are, for many, the most consoling words of our Lord Jesus. They are consoling because they acknowledge a reality that we so often try to hide: We are burdened and exhausted by the cares of life. And these burdens have, despite our best efforts to seek relief—and often because of them—made us weary. Because of this, what we want is rest. What we want is true peace. Somehow, we want to know that despite how things appear, all will be made well.

It is deeply consoling to know that Jesus recognizes this, He knows what we need, and He offers us a solution: Himself.

The problem is, I think, that we keep seeking to relieve these problems not in Him, but elsewhere. It reminds me of this really interesting verse in the Gospel of Luke:

> Be careful, or your hearts will be weighed
> down with carousing, drunkenness and
> the anxieties of life. (Luke 21:34)

I say *interesting* because if you think about it, the very reason we get drunk, that we go about carousing, that we are addicted to our news feeds and political podcasts, is precisely to find relief from our heavy hearts. And yet Our Lord tells us plainly to be careful of these things, because they will cause our hearts to be weighed down. What we seek as a cure (i.e., carousing, drunkenness, and the cares of this life) is actually making the disease worse.

The solution, Our Lord tells us, will not be found in any of these things the world puts forth, but instead will be found in Him. He alone can give us the peace that our hearts long for because He made our hearts. He knows us inside and out. And to quote St. Augustine's opening prayer to God from his *Confessions*, "Our hearts are restless until they rest in You."[1]

That's what this book is about. It's about taking Christ seriously when He says that rest is possible when we turn to Him for refuge. Christ did not come to merely help us cope with the anxieties of life. He came to give us peace. He came to be our refuge. That is the heart of this book.

---

[1] St. Augustine, The *Confessions of St. Augustine* (Image, 1960).

Peace I leave with you; my peace I give you. I do not give to you as the world gives. Do not let your hearts be troubled and do not be afraid.
John 14:27

Matt Fradd
Solemnity of the
Most Sacred Heart of Jesus
2025

Part I
Jesus, the Face of Mercy

Chapter 1

The Revelation of the Father's Love

Let all who take refuge in You be glad; let them ever sing for joy.
Psalm 5:11

Being Christian is not the result of an ethical choice or a lofty idea, but the encounter with an event, a person, which gives life a new horizon and a decisive direction.
Pope Benedict XVI, *Deus Caritas Est*

B y the time I was fourteen, I considered myself agnostic about God and Christianity. I had come to see belief in God as a psychological crutch—a comforting story that fragile people told themselves to take the edge off death. At the time, I thought this was an impressively mature insight. It felt clever.

Whenever I found myself in a conversation with a Christian, I'd toss out questions that sounded deep and unanswerable. "Oh yeah," I'd say, "well, who created God?" I now realize how unserious that question really was. After all, Christians don't believe that God is a created being. Quite the opposite: God is understood to be a metaphysical necessity—the uncaused cause, the unconditioned ground of all existence. Asking "Who created God?" is like asking, "If your brother is a bachelor, what's his wife's name?" It's a category mistake masquerading as insight.

At the time, I had a whole toolbox of these so-called "gotcha" questions. And I used them liberally.

But three years later, something changed.

At seventeen, I went on a trip to Rome for World Youth Day, the massive event hosted by St. John Paul II in the Great Jubilee Year 2000. I didn't go in search of spiritual truth. I wasn't hoping for a religious experience or trying to get closer to God. My reasons were simpler, more human: It was a free trip to Italy. And there were bound to be girls there.

Many of the other young people on the trip, though, *were* there for religious reasons. And to my surprise, they weren't the stereotypes I had expected. They were intelligent, joyful, attractive—and they believed in God without embarrassment. I didn't understand it.

Up until that point, the Christians I'd encountered hadn't made much of an impression. Their faith had always seemed tame and uninspiring—mostly sentimental fluff, vague moral encouragement with little to no philosophical depth. I had come to think of Christ, if

I thought of Him at all, as little more than a moral teacher from a bygone era. He was a figure locked away in stained glass and dust-covered statues. He felt distant. Irrelevant. Lifeless.

But in Rome, surrounded by these young Christians, I encountered something that felt different. Something more substantial. Something real. These weren't Christians simply because their parents were, or because they hadn't thought things through. Their faith had depth. It was personal. I didn't know what to do with that.

At first, I defaulted to my usual tactic: I asked my clever-sounding questions—the same tired objections I'd used before. But they didn't laugh at me or brush me off. They answered with patience and conviction. And eventually, I began to ask something else. Something deeper. I began to pray—not eloquently, just honestly. I said, "God, if You exist, would You reveal Yourself to me in a way that I can understand?"

And to my astonishment, He did.

God answered that prayer—mercifully and unmistakably. On that trip, I came to believe He existed, and He loved me as I was—even better, He loved me too much to leave me that way.

I encountered the person of Jesus Christ. And though it's difficult to put into words, the experience was like stepping into color for the first time. Everything around me seemed to pulse with meaning and beauty, as if the world had suddenly come alive.

When I returned home to Australia, I was one of those Christians who's so enthusiastic, so happy, that it almost makes you sick. I had fallen in love with Christ. It felt as though grace were being poured over me in waves. My old vices—still present, still persistent—began to lose their grip. I knew Jesus. I loved Jesus. And perhaps more astonishingly, I knew He knew and loved me.

Christianity Is Not a Philosophy

In my travels over the years, engaging with the Church in many places and across many cultures, I've noticed a troubling pattern—one that strikes at the very heart of Christianity. Far too many Christians treat their faith as little more than a system of morality.

Let me explain.

The great English Catholic apologist G.K. Chesterton was drawn to the faith, in large part, through the example of St. Francis of Assisi. Chesterton admired Francis deeply—so much so that one of the first books he published after his conversion was a biography of the saint.

He saw in Francis a man who had turned the world upside down by his radical embrace of poverty, humility, and joy. Francis didn't merely believe certain truths—he lived them. Chesterton famously described him as "a poet whose whole life was a poem."[2]

But perhaps the most striking line comes at the very beginning of the book, where Chesterton writes that Francis did not treat religion as a theory

---

[2] G.K. Chesterton, *St. Francis of Assisi* (New York: Image Books, 1924), 89.

or abstract idea. For him, it was something far more intimate. In Chesterton's words, "his religion was not a thing like a theory but a thing like a love-affair."[3] Indeed, I believe that all Christians would benefit from letting their religion be less of a syllogism and more of a love affair.

Chesterton's words deserve to be proclaimed from every pulpit. His insight touches something essential—something many of us have forgotten.

When Christianity is reduced to a syllogism or moral system, it loses its vitality. It becomes a cold ethic rather than a living encounter. And while you can still hear echoes of truth in it, the heart of the Gospel gets buried beneath abstractions.

You can see this reductionism in the way many Christians talk about the faith—as if Christianity were solely about right behavior and right thinking. The assumption often goes something like this: If only the world would stop fornicating, if people would stop being racist, if they would just follow the Church's moral teachings—then our families, our communities, and even our nations would flourish. These arguments rely on tidy syllogisms that attempt to change people's behavior, as if the world's brokenness stemmed simply from the wrong premises and conclusions.

But Christianity is not simply a system of ethics, nor is it a flawless chain of reasoning. It is not, at

---

[3] G.K Chesterton, *Francis of Assisi* (London: Hodder and Stoughton, 1923), 16.

its core, about compliance or intellectual assent. Christianity is about a Person. It is about love. A love that calls us, transforms us, and never leaves us the same.

Now, to be clear—Christianity is still *true*. It offers the most coherent and compelling vision of morality the world has ever seen. We have good arguments for God's existence. Our moral framework outshines any secular alternative. And the Church's teachings, especially on human dignity and sexuality, are not arbitrary—they are radiant with wisdom.

But here's the thing: We don't need divine revelation just to know that God exists or that we should live moral lives. Philosophy alone can take us surprisingly far. The ancient Greeks—Socrates, Plato, Aristotle, and others—understood much about virtue, truth, and even the necessity of a first cause and an Unmoved Mover (God).

And yet, Christianity offers something infinitely more. Our faith is not centered on an idea—it is centered on Christ. On a living person. Our hope is not grounded in a theory of the good life, but in the love of a God who stepped into history, took on flesh, knows us by name, and calls us into communion with Himself.

This is the God I met in Rome in the year 2000. While I was avoiding him with flimsy rationalizations, the Living God came and met me. He opened my eyes to see.

Jesus Reveals the Father

Humanity has always struggled to see God. And this struggle isn't limited to skeptics or nonbelievers. Even many faithful, practicing Christians have a distorted image of who God is and who He desires to be for us.

Some view God as a distant, disapproving Father—someone who might love us, but only out of obligation. He may forgive, yes, but only so many times. Beneath it all, we suspect He's disappointed, maybe even annoyed, and that eventually, His patience will run out.

Others imagine that God's affection is reserved for a select few—the saints, the virtuous, the people who seem to have their lives together. And so, if we're honest, we see ourselves as background characters in God's story. We think that He might tolerate us, but He certainly doesn't delight in us. We assume He's too busy with the important people to care about someone like us.

These misunderstandings are not simply emotional wounds or cultural misunderstandings—they're spiritual consequences of original sin. From the very first pages of Scripture, we're told that sin entered the world and disfigured our relationship with God. We should never lose sight of that reality. The messiness of the world today is not God's doing; it is our own. The messiness of original sin distorts our vision, placing us in a kind of spiritual fog. Like Adam and Eve, we hide from God, convinced He is someone to be feared, not someone to be loved.

St. Bonaventure, one of the great minds of the Church, reflected deeply on this condition. In *The Soul's Journey into God*, he writes that original sin has filled "the mind with ignorance and the flesh with concupiscence. As a result, man, blinded and bent over, sits in darkness and does not see the light of heaven unless grace with justice come to his aid…"[4]

That light of heaven, Bonaventure tells us, is not found in an idea or a moral code. In our "blinded and bent over state," it comes through a person: Jesus Christ.

Jesus did not come into the world to teach us a theory. He came to reveal a love—the kind of love that casts out fear, restores the image of God in our souls, and draws us into the very heart of God.

One of the most astonishing statements Jesus ever made is found in John 14:9: "He who has seen me has seen the Father." With these words, Jesus shattered any notion that God is distant, abstract, or unknowable. To know Christ is to know the Father. Through a relationship with Him, we begin to recover from the spiritual blindness caused by sin. We come to see that the heart of God is not cold or remote—but full of mercy, tenderness, and intimate love.

---

[4] St. Bonaventure, *The Soul's Journey to God* (New York: Paulist Press, 1978), 62.

We often wonder: *Does God really know me?* Not just in a general sense, but personally—with my anxieties, my hopes, my fears, my wounds. The answer, according to Jesus, is a resounding "yes"! "Even the hairs of your head are all counted," He tells us (Matthew 10:30). God knows us not just because He is all-knowing, but also because He is all-loving. His knowledge is not detached or clinical—it is personal, particular, and full of care.

The God Who Is Love

When St. John—the great Apostle and evangelist—described himself, he chose this phrase *the disciple whom Jesus loved.*

John was the youngest of the Twelve, likely only sixteen when he first encountered Jesus. He was still a boy by ancient standards, and yet Christ called him to a task of enormous magnitude. Despite his youth, John became one of the Lord's closest companions.

Perhaps this is why Jesus extended to him such special intimacy: John was invited up Mount Tabor to witness the Transfiguration, welcomed to lean against Christ's chest at the Last Supper, and called into the garden of Gethsemane to pray with the Lord in His hour of agony.

John's love for Christ was unwavering. And nowhere is this more clearly seen than at the foot of the Cross. When the other Apostles fled in fear, John stayed. He alone stood with Jesus in His final moments. According to tradition, John lived well into old age, dying around AD 100. That means he spent more than seventy years after the Resurrection longing to see his beloved Friend again. For a heart as devoted as his, such waiting was its own kind of suffering, a quiet martyrdom.

During a time of intense persecution against the early Christians, John was exiled to the island of Patmos. Isolated from the Church he loved, he found consolation in staying connected through letters. He wrote to encourage the faithful, to strengthen the Church from afar. Some of those letters became part of the New Testament.

In one of his final letters to the early Church, St. John wrote a line he had surely pondered and prayed over for decades: "God is love" (1 John 4:8).

Notice he didn't say that God is lovable or lovely or loving—although of course He is. He said God is love. Love is not something God does; it is who He is.

To deepen this understanding, we can turn to another apostle—St. Paul. In his famous passage on love in 1 Corinthians 13:4–8, Paul describes love with remarkable clarity and beauty. Though he may not have known John would one day write, "God is love," Paul was, in effect, describing God Himself. If John is right—and he is—then we can rephrase Paul's words this way:

> God is patient. God is kind. God is not
> envious or boastful or arrogant or

rude. God does not insist on His own
way. God is not irritable or resentful.
God does not rejoice in wrongdoing
but rejoices in the truth. God bears all
things, believes all things, hopes all
things, endures all things. God never
ends.

That is good news! In fact, it's the best news we
could ever receive: Jesus Christ has revealed to us
not just that God exists, but also who He is and
what He is really like.

But here's something we often forget: Good
news without bad news is often seen as no news.

Imagine that a fireman bursts into your house at
six in the morning, wakes your entire family, and
shouts, "Don't worry—there's no fire!" You'd be
confused, even angry. Why this intrusion? Why the
panic? But now imagine the opposite: There *is* a fire.
The house is moments away from collapse. The fireman breaks down the door, pulls you and your
family to safety, and saves your life. Suddenly, that
same intrusion becomes the greatest gift imaginable.

The point is this: The Gospel is only truly understood and fully appreciated in light of the bad
news it overcomes.

The message that God is love is radiant and
true—but it can sound hollow or unnecessary if we
don't first understand what has gone wrong. And
that's precisely what we've neglected. For decades—especially since the 1960s—we've often

hesitated to speak about sin, judgment, death, and the devil. But the Gospel is only fully understood when we are honest about the darkness it came to conquer. And a refuge only matters when we reckon with the dangers outside.

Something very dreadful and very real is lurking at the door.

Chapter 2

The Searching Shepherd

For the Son of Man came to seek and save the lost.
Luke 19:10

J esus revealed to us that the Father is love—and in doing so, He also revealed who He Himself is. Among the many names He used, one of the most tender and profound is the "Good Shepherd." We find this revelation in the Gospel of John, when Jesus states: "I am the good shepherd. . . The good shepherd lays down his life for the sheep" (John 10:11, 14).

The image of the Lord as Shepherd held a special place in the hearts of the first Jewish Christians, echoing the beloved words of Psalm 23. Even today, this remains one of the most treasured passages in all of Scripture. It begins with these familiar words:

> The Lord is my shepherd, I shall not want.
> He makes me lie down in green pastures;
> he leads me beside still waters;
> he restores my soul.

Psalm 23 must have brought consolation to many of the early Christians who were persecuted and martyred for the faith. These early Christians often portrayed Jesus as the Good Shepherd in their art. One of the oldest known depictions is a third-century image found on the walls of the St. Callistus Catacomb in Rome, where Jesus is shown carrying a lamb on His shoulders.

Beyond this beautiful imagery, our Lord Jesus added deeper layers of meaning. He didn't choose the image of the shepherd merely because it is tender and peaceful. His purposes seem to be twofold.

First, He shows us that, as the Good Shepherd, He is willing to lay down His life to protect His sheep. He is good because He is protective. In the Gospel of John, Jesus says:

> I am the good shepherd. The good shepherd lays down his life for the sheep. The hired hand is not the shepherd and does not own the sheep. So when he sees the

wolf coming, he abandons the sheep and runs away. Then the wolf attacks the flock and scatters it. The man runs away because he is a hired hand and cares nothing for the sheep. (John 10:11–13)

The second purpose of the image is to show that God actively seeks out His sheep. Jesus is the Good Shepherd because He is willing to risk everything to find each and every one:

Which one of you, having a hundred sheep and losing one of them, does not leave the ninety-nine in the wilderness and go after the one that is lost until he finds it? When he has found it, he lays it on his shoulders and rejoices. And when he comes home, he calls together his friends and neighbors, saying to them, 'Rejoice with me, for I have found my sheep that was lost.' Just so, I tell you, there will be more joy in heaven over one sinner who repents than over ninety-nine righteous persons who need no repentance. (Luke 15:4–7)

God is searching. Each of us needs the experience of being found by Him. As I shared in Chapter 1, I was once a lost agnostic, tangled up in sins that were both exhausting and ultimately unsatisfying—until God, my Good Shepherd, found me.

The Spiritual Meaning of the Fig Trees

In the Bible, God consistently seeks out the lost—and time and again, He finds them under fig trees. Fig trees appear frequently in Scripture and have come to symbolize the human experience of being found, seen, and mercifully forgiven by God.

Adam and Eve, after disobeying God, ran and hid among the trees of the garden (see Genesis 3). In their shame, they grabbed the nearest branches—fig leaves (Latin: *folia ficus*)—and tried to cover themselves, as if to hide their guilt from the One who made them. But there, under the fig tree, in the midst of their sin and fear, they were found by God.

Generations later, Zacchaeus—a sinful man living in the corrupt city of Jericho—climbed a "sycamore-fig tree" (Latin: *ficus sycomorus*) just to catch a glimpse of Jesus (see Luke 19). Interestingly, this variety of fig must be pierced before it becomes sweet and edible.[5] Zacchaeus, in a state of sin, used the fig tree to find God—and there, among the branches, he was called by God.

We also hear of Nathanael, who was once sitting under a fig tree (Latin: *sub ficu*) when Jesus saw him from afar. Scripture doesn't tell us what he was thinking or praying, but Jesus' words suggest that something profound had happened in Nathanael's heart. "Nathanael said to him, 'How do you know me?' Jesus answered him, 'Before

---

[5] See Pliny the Elder's *Natural History*.

Philip called you, when you were under the fig tree, I saw you.' Nathanael answered him, 'Rabbi, you are the Son of God! You are the King of Israel!'" (John 1:48–49). Perhaps, in that quiet moment under the tree, Nathanael had longed to be seen by God—and there, beneath the fig tree, he was.

For the Christian, these biblical stories of God's seeking and finding the lost are not merely relics of the past. The symbolism, the encounters, the mercy—they are meant to overflow into our own lives. Just as they did for St. Augustine, who found himself pursued and embraced by the God who still seeks us.

St. Augustine Is Finally Found

A moment beneath a fig tree marked a turning point in the conversion of the great Catholic saint, Augustine. St. Augustine is one of the most relatable saints for men and women today. Though he lived in the fourth and fifth centuries and belonged to the ancient Church, his spiritual journey—especially as told in *The Confessions*—has a surprisingly modern tone and emotional honesty.

In many ways, we are not so different from Augustine. Most people today have at least heard of Jesus. They've been told—perhaps in passing—that they should try to be good, and that believing in Jesus is the path to heaven. And yet, many find it hard to care. There's a kind of spiritual apathy that marks our age. It's part of the postmodern predicament: Western society often greets the Gospel not with outrage or curiosity, but with a shrug—as if to say, "Been there, done that."

In this, St. Augustine was very much like us. Like many today, Augustine struggled with disordered desires and the pull of worldly pleasures. He was entangled in sexual sin, kept a mistress for years, fathered a child out of wedlock, and was caught up in the "bread and circuses" of Roman culture—seeking distraction, intellectual advancement, and entertainment instead of truth and virtue.

In *The Confessions*, he writes with striking honesty about his inner conflict. He knew what was right, but he couldn't bring himself to choose it. He went back and forth, unable to make a decisive commitment to moral virtue or to God. Though he knew about Jesus, he simply didn't care.

Augustine's autobiographical writing slowly reveals that the real story unfolding is not so much about Augustine's search for God, but about God's relentless pursuit of Augustine. He was the lost sheep—and Jesus, the Good Shepherd, was determined to find him. In this pursuit Augustine was also blessed with a saintly mother, St. Monica, who never stopped calling him to a higher standard—and never stopped loving him unconditionally.

That moment of being found came on a fateful day when Augustine was in deep misery. Resisting God, clinging to sin, and chasing after pleasure had left him empty. The life of indulgence and distraction was no longer satisfying—it was making him sad. And yet, the idea of leaving it all behind for the Christian way of life filled him with fear.

He writes:

> When a deep consideration had from the secret bottom of my soul drawn together and heaped up all my misery in the sight of my heart; there arose a mighty storm, bringing a mighty shower of tears. . . . I cast myself down I know not how, under a certain *fig-tree*, giving full vent to my tears; and the floods of mine eyes gushed out an acceptable sacrifice to Thee.[6]

So, Augustine finds himself at the midpoint of his life, under a fig tree. It is there that God meets him in a powerful way. God speaks to him first through the voice of a child. Apparently, in a nearby neighbor's yard, a child was playing some kind of game.

He writes:

> So was I speaking and weeping in the most bitter contrition of my heart, when, lo! I heard from a neighboring house a voice, as of boy or girl, I know not,

---

[6] St. Augustine, *The Confessions of St. Augustine* (Image, 1960), Book VIII, Chapter XII, p. 202, italics added.

chanting, and oft repeating, 'Take up and read; Take up and read.' . . . Checking the torrent of my tears, I arose; interpreting it to be no other than a command from God to open the bible and read the first chapter I should find.[7]

Augustine rises from beneath the fig tree and finds a Bible. Desperate for direction, he opens it at random—what we might call a game of "Bible roulette." He goes on:

I seized, opened, and in silence read that section on which my eyes first fell: "Not in rioting and drunkenness, not in chambering and wantonness, not in strife and envying; but put ye on the Lord Jesus Christ, and make not provision for the flesh, in concupiscence." [Romans 13:13–14] No further would I read; nor needed I: for instantly at the end of this sentence, by a light as it were of serenity infused into my heart, all the darkness of doubt vanished away.[8]

Augustine allowed himself to be found by God,

---

[7] *The Confessions of St. Augustine*, Book VIII, Chapter XII, p 202.

[8] *The Confessions of St. Augustine*, Book VIII, Chapter XII, p 202 (brackets added).

opening his heart with honesty and a sincere desire to discover the truth about life. His story continues to shine a light for us today, reminding us of the importance of facing the truth about ourselves and the meaning of our lives.

The Bad News

God is searching. And that is very good news. But it raises an uncomfortable question: *Why* is He searching?

That's the bad news—it's because we are lost. Not just a little lost, like someone who's taken a wrong turn and needs a map. We are spiritually lost—eternally lost—apart from His grace. We are wounded, wretched, and doomed without Him.

This is not a small problem. It's not just that we need a little guidance or inspiration. We need rescuing. And Jesus, the Good Shepherd, has come precisely for that.

In today's world, many have a diluted image of Jesus. He's often presented as a gentle man with a soft voice, who encourages kindness and maybe a bit of recycling. When we hear that Jesus is the Good Shepherd, we hardly blink. But this image, properly understood, is anything but sentimental. It speaks to something profound and urgent.

First, it reminds us that we truly are lost. We are the sheep who have wandered far. And if we are not found, the end is not simply unfortunate—it is tragic. Sin leads to death, destruction, and eternal separation from God. It shatters our souls, harms our families, and disfigures everything it touches. Sin is not a myth. It is real. And it is ugly.

Second, it tells us that God is not only gentle but zealous. He seeks us out with tenacity to save us from destruction. He is not motivated by vengeance, but by love. Like a parent desperately searching for a lost child, God comes looking for us with a heart full of compassion. He wants us back—not to punish, but to rescue.

The State of the World

Since the 1960s, Western society has steadily drifted away from God. The Christian vision of life—once the foundation of culture and meaning—was gradually replaced by a postmodern,[9] secular worldview. But the promises of postmodernity have proven hollow. The answers it offers have turned out to be no answers at all. The evidence of this failure is everywhere: in fractured families, rising despair, and any number of haunting movements that mark our age.

Postmodern thought has collapsed under its own weight. And until the Christian worldview is renewed—until Christ is once again recognized as the one, true refuge—the world will continue to groan under a sorrow so deep, it feels almost apocalyptic.

---

[9] For an in-depth review of postmodern thought, see Noelle Mering, *Awake, Not Woke: A Christian Response to the Cult of Progressive Ideology* (Tan Books, 2021).

Looking over recent social statistics reveals a society unraveling at the seams. It is crushing to think that the numbers are not simply data points, but that they represent real people, each carrying silent burdens and suffering untold anguish. Let's take a quick look at some telling statistics, each of which is in some way a consequence of sin.

According to the Centers for Disease Control and Prevention (CDC), approximately 49,300 people in the United States died by suicide last year—that's roughly one person every ten minutes. The suicide rate among men was nearly four times that of women. Even more alarming is the rising rate among children aged eight to twelve, which has climbed steadily over the past fifteen years. Despair, it seems, is reaching even the youngest hearts.[10]

Divorce continues to tear at the fabric of God's design for the family. The CDC reported in 2023 that roughly 40 to 45 percent of first marriages in the United States end in divorce, amounting to around 689,000 divorces annually. Behind those numbers lie countless broken vows and fractured homes. While the divorce rate has declined in recent years, this is not because marriage is thriving—it's because fewer young people are getting married at all. In a culture that prizes autonomy over

---

[10] See Centers for Disease Control and Prevention, "Suicide Deaths, Plans, and Attempts in the United States," March 26, 2025, https://www.cdc.gov/suicide/facts/data.html.

covenant, many now drift alone, seeking fulfillment in individualism rather than the unity God intended.[11]

Abortion adds yet another layer to this tragedy. According to the Guttmacher Institute, there were an estimated 1.026 million abortions in the United States in 2023. Each of these children—knit together in the womb by God (see Psalm 139:13)—was denied the gift of life in a world that often favors convenience over creation. The Catholic Church reminds us of the sacredness of every human life (*CCC*, 2270), a truth rejected every time this silent violence takes place.[12]

The crisis deepens with the widespread use of drugs, revealing the ache of a culture in flight from reality. The CDC reports that drug overdose deaths in 2023 reached 107,543. In addition, the National Survey on Drug Use and Health (NSDUH) found that 29.5 million Americans aged twelve and older suffer from substance use disorders. From a Christian perspective, this surge is the bitter fruit of a society hurting and in pain, disconnected from truth, and seeking escape in chemical illusions rather than in the healing refuge of Christ.[13]

---

[11] National Center for Health Statistics, "Marriages and Divorces," https://www.cdc.gov/nchs/nvss/marriage-divorce.htm.

[12] https://www.guttmacher.org/fact-sheet/induced-abortion-united-states.

[13] See Matthew F. Garnett, MPH, and Arialdi M. Miniño, MPH, *Drug Overdose Deaths in the United States, 2003–*

Crime, too, reflects the consequences of moral and familial breakdown. According to the FBI's Uniform Crime Reporting (UCR) data for 2023, there were more than 1.2 million violent acts: murders, assaults, rapes and robberies. This lawlessness is illustrative of deep spiritual wounds.[14]

Perhaps most devastating of all is the crisis of fatherlessness—a silent epidemic. The U.S. Census Bureau estimates that 18.4 million children—one in four—live without a biological, step, or adoptive father in the home. The absence of fathers leaves countless children without guidance, protection, or love from a man who reflects God's own fatherly heart.[15]

Together, these statistics paint a picture of humanity unmoored from its Creator. The *Catechism of the Catholic Church* rightly warns that turning from God leads to "a kingdom of death" (*CCC*, 1008). And here it is before us: lives ended, families shattered, innocence lost.

It becomes clear, then, why Jesus calls Himself the Good Shepherd—the one who searches for the

---

2023, Centers for Disease Control and Prevention, https://www.cdc.gov/nchs/data/databriefs/db522.pdf.
[14] https://cde.ucr.cjis.gov/LATEST/webapp/#/pages/home.
[15] Jack Brewer, *Fatherlessness and Its Effects on American Society*, May 15 2023, https://www.americafirstpolicy.com/assets/uploads/files/Issue_Breif_-_Fatherlessness_and_its_effects_on_American_society.pdf.

lost. Because we *are* lost without Him. And unless we let ourselves be found, the sorrow of this world will only deepen.

Drawing the Battle Lines

What are we to do?

We must throw ourselves before the seat of Mercy. There, before Christ, we find our only true refuge.

And then—strengthened by grace and moved by love—we must face the spiritual battle unfolding around us. This battle is threefold: against the devil, the flesh, and the world.

Most serious Christians have at least a moderate understanding of the devil. They know he is real—a personal enemy. Scripture reveals him as a fallen angel, the "father of lies" (John 8:44), who, along with his fellow demons, labors with relentless malice to twist souls away from salvation.

Serious Christians also recognize the battle against the flesh—our own fallen nature. They understand the internal war with gluttony, lust, pride, and other disordered passions that blind us, cloud our judgment, and leave us vulnerable to greater sins.

But when it comes to the third enemy—the world—many believers are less clear. The term often feels vague or misunderstood.

Scripture uses the word *world* in at least three distinct ways:

- First, it can refer to creation itself—God's handiwork—which He declared "very good" (Genesis 1:31).
- Second, it can mean humanity: "For God so loved the world, that He gave His only begotten Son" (John 3:16).
- Third, and most crucial for understanding spiritual warfare, it can refer to sinful society—the collective rebellion against God. This is what St. James means when he warns: "Anyone who chooses to be a friend of the world becomes an enemy of God" (James 4:4).

These three enemies—the devil, the flesh, and the world—often work together. Deceitful ideas (the devil) that play to disordered desires (the flesh) that are normalized by a sinful society (the world). The world normalizes and even celebrates deceitful ideas that play to disordered desires.

Take the example of a man who wants to commit adultery. He may come to believe that monogamy is unnatural and impossible, which plays into his disordered desire for sexual pleasure. This is then normalized by a sinful society that says, "You only live once—you should do what makes you happy."

Yet in the midst of this spiritual battlefield, God continues to search. He searched for Adam and Eve. He called Zacchaeus from a tree. He saw Nathanael under the fig tree. He pursued Augustine until the moment of surrender.

For each of them, a life-changing encounter happened—symbolically or literally—in the shade of a fig tree.

Still today, God searches for us. For us, too, the light of God can break through the shadow of sin that hangs over our lives. But we must step out. We must come out from behind, from beneath, or from within whatever "fig tree" we're hiding under.

We must let God find us.

Chapter 3

Lord of All

I am the way, and the truth, and the life.
No one comes to the Father except through me.
John 14:6

R ecently, I had an experience in prayer that I
want to share with you. I had gotten up early
and was spending time communing with the Lord.
These early mornings of prayer are such a gift to
me, especially on days that are shaping up to be
full and busy—and this was one of those days.
That morning, my prayer was a blend of two
things: reflecting on the Scripture readings for the
day and considering what lay ahead.

Here is what I believe God said to me: "My good son, I love you. You're doing a good job and I'm proud of you."

There was something about those words—they came out of nowhere and struck me, like a sudden wake-up call from deep sleep. They rattled me, not with fear, but with a kind of startling kindness I didn't know what to do with.

You'd think those would be the most consoling words to hear from God, right? But for some reason, I recoiled at the sheer kindness in the Father's voice. It caught me off guard. Part of me wanted to push the words away, to question them, even to disprove them. I was pretty sure I could.

"No, God," I might have said, "You're thinking of someone else. I'm not that Matthew. I'm not that good or worthy of being loved."

After that inner recoil, I had to pause and say to myself: "That's weird. Why did I respond like that?" The Holy Spirit has a gentle, persistent way of drawing us into deeper questions. And in that moment, I sensed Him nudging me, almost playfully: "Interesting that you reacted that way—why do you think you do that?"

It was a question worth sitting with. And I don't think I'm alone in it—maybe anyone earnestly trying to grow closer to God has felt something similar.

Why did it feel like I would've preferred God to scold me rather than speak with such tenderness? Was I afraid that if He were too kind, I'd lose my motivation to strive harder in my spiritual life? It's easier, somehow, to picture God as One who demands much, asks much, judges much. But to imagine Him loving us deeply, liking us tenderly, forgiving us freely, and speaking to us with kindness—that's the real challenge.

I wrestled with those thoughts for a few days. And then, unexpectedly, St. Thérèse of Lisieux came to mind, and with her, a kind of clarity.

Near the end of her life, Thérèse—this little soul who had walked such a hidden path of trust—summed up her whole journey with these simple, stunning words: "I believe in Your love for me, and I believe in my love for You."[16]

These are profound belief statements. It's one thing to accept that God loves us in some general, theological sense—but far harder to believe that He actually likes us.

Isn't it true that we often feel we need to be perfect before we can come to God? Like we have to fix ourselves first—pull it together, clean up the mess, and then approach Him.

But thankfully, I've come to see that this is completely backward. In fact, it's a godless way of thinking. God doesn't ask us to come once we've solved our problems—He invites us to come *with* them. With our brokenness. With our misery. That's the very place where His love meets us.

Because the truth is, it's only when we know we are

---

[16] Fr. Jean C.J. D'Elbee, *I Believe in Love: A Personal Retreat Based on the Teaching of St. Thérèse of Lisieux* (Sophia Institute Press, 2001), 78.

loved—and begin to believe in that love—that we can finally open up the hidden closets of the soul, let the light in, and begin to heal.

Jesus Asks Us a Question

As we read through Matthew's Gospel and follow the words and actions of Christ, we eventually come to a moment—about halfway through—when Jesus turns and asks *us*, the readers, a question.

The scene takes place as Jesus traveled north from Galilee to Caesarea Philippi—the northernmost point in the Holy Land where we know He walked. It's there, in this remote and significant setting, that Jesus paused to speak with His disciples. He asked them two questions.

The first was this: "Who do people say that the Son of Man is?" (Matthew 16:13).

The disciples had differing answers. They spoke about what others were saying—some believed Jesus was John the Baptist, while others said Elijah or one of the prophets.

But Jesus wasn't just taking a poll. He wanted something deeper. He turned the question inward, directing it straight to them—to their hearts. And so He asked: "But who do you say that I am?" (Matthew 16:15).

Then, it became personal. And as we read this moment in Scripture, the spotlight shifts—it's no longer just a question for the disciples. It's a question for *us*.

The Bible is not a dead text—it is living and active, inspired by God Himself. That means when Jesus asks, "Who do you say that I am?" He is asking you and me, here and now.

So pause for a moment and consider it honestly: *Who is Jesus to me?*

Our culture offers no shortage of opinions about Jesus. But many of them share one common flaw: They strip Him of His divinity. They reduce Him to something more manageable, less threatening. A historical figure, a moral teacher, a revolutionary, a myth—anything but the Son of God.

Some see Jesus as simply a *moral teacher*—a wise man who preached love, especially love of neighbor, but nothing more. In this view, His words are inspiring, but He is not divine.

Others portray Him as a *political revolutionary*—a kind of first-century activist who challenged the power structures of His day, siding with the poor and calling for radical social change.

Still others claim Jesus is just a *myth or symbol*. Virtually every serious scholar has refuted this, such as Dr. Brant Pitre in his book *The Case for Jesus*.[17] Even agnostics such as Dr. Bart Ehrman[18] have had to admit that Jesus was a real historical figure. But even still, some cling to the idea that Jesus is only a patchwork of ancient legends, perhaps borrowed from figures like the Egyptian god Horus, molded

---

[17] Brant Pitre, *The Case for Jesus: The Biblical and Historical Evidence for Christ* (Image, 2016).

[18] Bart Ehrman, *Did Jesus Exist? The Historical Argument for Jesus of Nazareth* (Harper One, 2013).

into a fictional character meant to inspire moral living.

And finally, some argue Jesus was merely an *apocalyptic Jewish rabbi*—a man concerned with end-times speculation, but never one who claimed to be the Messiah, let alone God Himself.

Each of these responses, in its own way, falls short. They misunderstand Him. They attempt to explain Jesus while avoiding the uncomfortable truth of His divinity.

In Caesarea Philippi, it was St. Peter who gave the correct answer: "You are the Messiah, the Son of the living God" (Matthew 16:16).

But how did Peter come to this understanding of who Jesus truly was? It wasn't through mere reasoning or secondhand opinions. It was born out of an experience—a moment that unfolded earlier, on the Sea of Galilee, in the heart of a storm. Let's take a moment to reflect on that scene, meditating on the moment Peter quite literally fell into the arms of God.

The Storm on the Sea of Galilee

St. Peter's life with Jesus is so relevant to us today because his story is full of highs and lows. It's beautifully human and divine all at once.

In the Gospels, Peter often comes across as impulsive—the kind of man who speaks and acts before thinking things through. He's quick to jump in, and because of that, he often ends up putting his proverbial foot in his mouth.

But here's the beauty: When Peter places that same boldness and enthusiasm at the service of Jesus, we begin to see the man who would become a saint.

In the episode we're reflecting on, evening had come. Jesus and the disciples had spent the day among large crowds, and now Jesus began dismissing them. That must have taken some time.

But this evening, Jesus had something in mind. You might say He was up to something. Matthew tells us: "Immediately, Jesus made the disciples get into the boat and go on ahead to the other side, while He dismissed the crowds" (Matthew 14:22).

The disciples obeyed. They didn't know exactly why they were separating from Jesus. Maybe they asked one another what He was planning to do.

The next stage of this episode finds Jesus alone on the shore, praying. Meanwhile, the disciples were miles away, caught in a storm. The clouds had rolled in, and the wind and waves were picking up speed and strength. The boat was straining against the water, and the disciples—seasoned fishermen though some of them were—began to fear.

We should pause here and recognize something important: Jesus *knew* the storm was coming. He could have delayed their departure; he could have waited for calmer weather. But instead, He sent them out—at what seems like the worst possible moment.

Why? Because Jesus had a plan.

The One who rules the wind and the sea is also the One who *created* them. Every gust of wind and crashing wave that has ever existed was already in the mind of God at the dawn of time. This particular storm wasn't an accident—it was divinely prepared.

Jesus intended to use it—not to punish, but to teach and form. This storm is part of how He would shape His disciples into the saints, apostles, and martyrs they were destined to become.

As the night deepened and the storm raged, Jesus began to move. Picture Him now, stepping out onto the water. The waves crashed around Him, but He walked steadily, calmly, directly toward His disciples. He did not run. He did not panic.

Jesus is Lord. He is Master of time and destiny. He *is* Peace. Time belongs to Him. This has been so for Our Lord since the beginning of time, where the book of Genesis tells us: "The Spirit of God moved over the waters" (Genesis 1:2).

As Jesus slowly emerged from the darkness, the disciples caught sight of a figure walking on the water—and they were terrified. In their fear, they didn't recognize Him. To their eyes, He looked like a ghost, a phantom rising out of the storm.

But their terror wasn't just from exhaustion or panic. It was the simple, startling fact that mere men don't walk on water. What they were witnessing defied everything they knew about reality. And in the middle of an already overwhelming storm, this only added to their dread.

They believed they were about to die—and the spirit coming to claim them had them fully convinced.

But then Jesus spoke. His voice cut through the

wind—calm, steady, and unmistakable: "Take courage. It is I. Do not be afraid." (Matthew 14:27).

And here's what's striking: He didn't command the storm to stop—not yet. He commanded *their fear* to stop. He addressed not the sea, but their hearts. Shouldn't He have calmed the waves first?

Apparently not. Because the greater danger in that moment wasn't around them—it was within them.

And even more mysteriously, Jesus didn't walk straight up to the boat. He stopped a short distance away.

That's the moment Peter did something remarkable. Recognizing the Lord, he decided he would rather be in the storm with Jesus than safe in the boat without Him.

And so Peter said, "Lord, if it is you, command me to come to you on the water" (Matthew 14:28).

Jesus responded with a simple invitation: "Come."

The eternal Son of God stood upon the waves, and Peter—this impulsive, fearful fisherman—stepped out of the boat to join Him. Now they were both walking toward each other across the storm. But then Peter faltered. He took his eyes off Jesus and looked instead at the wind and the waves.

"When he noticed the strong wind, he became frightened, and beginning to sink, he cried out, 'Lord, save me!'" (Matthew 14:30).

As he began to go under, helpless and afraid, Peter turned his eyes back to Jesus—who now stood before him not just as teacher, but as Savior.

"Jesus immediately reached out his hand and caught him, saying, 'You of little faith, why did you doubt?'" (Matthew 14:31).

Peter may have been sinking, but grace had the final word. In that moment of desperation, he returned his gaze to Jesus—and there, in the arms of God, he found refuge and salvation.

It's because of this moment on the sea that Peter was later able to stand with confidence at Caesarea Philippi and proclaim to the world: "You are the Christ, the Son of the living God" (Matthew 16:16).

That bold confession didn't come from theory or hearsay—it came from his experience and the Father's revelation. Peter believed it with every fiber of his being, because he had *lived* it. He had seen the divinity of Christ revealed on the Sea of Galilee.

And when the storm finally calmed, what seemed like a terrifying ordeal was revealed to be a divine gift. In that storm, the disciples didn't just witness Jesus' power as He walked on water or silenced the wind—they received their first taste of salvation. They didn't just hear about being saved. They *felt* it. They *saw* it. They *lived* it.

We need to encounter Christ as *our* Savior—not just as a theological truth, but as a personal reality. It's one thing to say, "Jesus redeemed the human race." It's another to say, with conviction: "He saved me. He saved you." That changes everything. That heals the soul.

Think about it: Healing, forgiveness, mercy—these are things nearly everyone, Christian or not, would agree are good and desirable.

But here's the catch: To be saved, we must first recognize we're in desperate need. To be healed, we have to admit we're sick. To be forgiven, we must own our sin. To receive mercy, we have to come as weak and broken.

And yet—these are often the very things we resist. We don't want to be seen as lost, fragile, or in need. We'd rather be the helper than the helped, the strong than the needy. But until we see ourselves as the ones in need of rescue, we can't truly encounter the One who came to save.

So it's no surprise that page after page of the Gospels seem written precisely to convince us of this truth—that *we* are the ones He came to save.

This was God's complaint against the Christians in Laodicea:

> For you say, 'I am rich, I have prospered, and I need nothing,' not realizing that you are wretched, pitiable, poor, blind, and naked. (Revelation 3:17)

They had forgotten their need for Christ. They believed they were fine on their own—strong, self-sufficient, in control. And in doing so, they had unknowingly placed themselves in the gravest spiritual danger.

If we claim that Jesus is a Savior but refuse to

admit that we need saving, then His salvation becomes meaningless to us. It's no longer Good News—it's no news at all.

But when we see clearly—when we recognize we are in a battle, wounded and weary and in need of rescue—then the Lordship of Jesus, and the refuge He offers, becomes the *greatest* news on earth.

Whatever storm you find yourself in today, remember this: Behind the wind and the waves stands the power of Christ—*and He is on your side*. He calls out to you. He walks with you.

When we proclaim, "Jesus is Lord," we're not only acknowledging His authority *over* us—we're declaring His protection, His faithfulness, and His deep, abiding love *for* us. He is everything a king is meant to be—just, strong, wise, and merciful.

But in this fallen world, under the shadow of original sin, we face an enemy who is always at work—the devil, who constantly seeks to distort our vision of God. He wants us to see Jesus not as the King of Mercy, but as a tyrant. Not as a Savior, but as a rival. A petty ruler who limits our freedom and holds power over us for His own gain.

But here's the good news: Yes, there is an enemy. But it's *not* Jesus. The *Catechism of the Catholic Church* says:

> Christ exercises his kingship by drawing all men to himself through his death and Resurrection. Christ, King and Lord of the universe, made himself the servant of all, for he came "not to be served but to

serve, and to give his life as a ransom for many." (*CCC*, 786)

Thankfully, Christ is on our side—and Christ is a warrior. Before Him, every knee shall bend (see Philippians 2:10). He is the One before whom demons tremble (see James 2:19). He is the One who went to the Cross for us, who descended into death to shatter the gates of hell, and who rose again in victory.

This is why He is Lord. And because He is divine, He alone can offer true refuge.

No other religious figure—whether Buddha, Muhammad, Joseph Smith, or Confucius—has ever claimed to personally offer eternal salvation. Only Jesus does. Only Jesus *can*.

Through the Scriptures, Jesus teaches us that what we need most is not an easy life. We don't need a God who hovers over us like a helicopter parent, nervously removing every obstacle.

We don't need a fussy God who exists merely to keep us comfortable.

What we need is a God who leads us into battle. A God who walks with us through the storms, through the wilderness, and into the Promised Land. A God whose strength is not shown by taking away every trial, but by *fighting through them alongside us*.

In this light, the refuge Jesus offers isn't a warm blanket that simply makes us feel better. It's a fortress. A place of strength. A wall at our back from which we can stand and fight. And here's the astonishing truth: Jesus doesn't need convincing to save us or love us—He already has, and He already is.

We don't need to fear Him or recoil from His kindness, as I did that morning in prayer.

We need to trust Him. To believe in His love. And though that may seem like a small step, when we finally do—when we entrust ourselves to Him in the middle of life's storms—we are not far from the Kingdom of God.

Chapter 4

Friend of Sinners

The Lord redeems His servants; no one
will be condemned who takes refuge in Him.
Psalm 34:22

I have called you friends.
John 15:15

I was eight years old when I first stumbled upon pornography. I wasn't looking for it. Like most boys that age, I didn't even understand what it was at first. It entered my life uninvited—an unwanted introduction to something that would prove poisonous. Don't get me wrong—I was fascinated. I was curious. Even excited by what I saw. But underneath all that, I still knew it was wrong.

Each of us is born with what I call a "moral nervous

system." Much like the biological nervous system, which regulates our bodies in relation to the *physical* world around us, the idea of a "moral nervous system" can be thought of as an internal framework that regulates our responses to the *moral* world around us.

That day, my eight-year-old moral nervous system kicked in. I felt a sense of shame and guilt. And I buried those feelings deep. I didn't talk about them—I didn't even know how.

I know I'm not alone in this. All of us, in one way or another, go looking for a false refuge. We try to fill the ache in our hearts with anything that promises to make us feel whole: drugs, alcohol, sex, money, power, fame. But these are cheap imitations of what we're really looking for. And the more we chase them, the more they wrap around us—tightening their grip, and slowly suffocating the soul.

Unholy Fears

Sin plants in us an unholy fear of God. But why? Why is our instinct, after falling, to run and hide— just like Adam and Eve in the Garden?

We are not so different from our first parents. We reach for spiritual fig leaves, stitching together makeshift coverings to hide our shame. We seek shelter among the trees, hoping the shadows will conceal what we cannot bear to face.

And yet, Jesus has revealed a God who is not only just but deeply merciful. A God who runs toward the sinner, not away from. Jesus told us that in Him we would find forgiveness, love, and rest for our weary souls. So, logically, after we've sinned, we should run straight to Him—the one place where the crushing weight of guilt is lifted. We should flee to Christ, our refuge.

But we don't.

Why?

Where does this distorted fear come from—the kind that makes us hide from the very One who can heal us?

The answer is both simple and profound. This unholy fear doesn't come from God—it comes from another source. Jesus calls the devil "the Accuser," and that title is no accident. The same ancient serpent who deceived Adam and Eve is still at work today, whispering lies into human hearts. He accuses, belittles, and fans the flames of a distorted fear that drives us away from the Father rather than toward Him. His goal has always been the same: to separate us from God, to thwart the plan of God, and to convince us that our sin makes us unlovable and that mercy is out of reach.

But Jesus' plan is entirely different. He doesn't push us away—He draws us close. He wants friendship with us, not fear. In fact, Our Lord went to the greatest lengths imaginable to prove this: by laying down His life in love. Through His Cross, He shows us once and for all that we never need to hide from Him. Instead, we can run to Him with confidence, knowing we'll be met not with condemnation but mercy. God knows our sin but calls us by name. The Accuser, on the other hand, knows our name—but calls us by our sin. One voice invites us into healing, the other into shame. The choice is ours: to listen to the lie that keeps us hiding, or to respond to the love that calls us home.

Fr. Jean d'Elbee makes this point beautifully when he writes:

> I assure you, *we are bathed in love and mercy*. We each have a Father, a brother, a Friend, a Spouse of our soul, Center and King of our hearts, Redeemer and Savior, bent down over us, over our weakness and our impotence, like that of little children, with an inexpressible gentleness, watching over us like the apple of His eye, who said, 'I will have mercy and not sacrifice, for I have not come to call the just, but sinners'; a Jesus haunted by the desire to save us by all means, who has opened Heaven under our feet. And we live, too often, like orphans, like abandoned children, as if it were Hell which had opened under our feet. We are men of little faith![19]

I love how Fr. Jean phrases this reality. Jesus opened for us the gates of heaven. And yet we run

---

[19] D'Elbee, *I Believe in Love*, 23 (italics added).

from God as though He's opening the gates of hell for us.

We should keep this passage close to our heart: "I do not call you servants any longer, because the servant does not know what the master is doing; but *I have called you friends*" (John 15:15, italics added).

The idea that we can be friends of God is one of the most profound revelations Jesus gave us—something worth returning to again and again, letting it sink deeper into our hearts and minds. I want to turn now to a passage from the Gospels where this truth comes to life. It's the story of a sinful man named Matthew, whose entire life was transformed the moment he became a friend of God.

The Tax Collector Saint

Matthew was a tax collector—and in biblical terms, that meant more than just an unpopular profession. He wasn't simply disliked; he was despised. Matthew had done the unthinkable: He had betrayed his own people and his faith by aligning himself with the Roman oppressors. To many faithful Jews, this made him a traitor, someone beyond forgiveness, someone to be avoided and excluded.

That's why what happened next must have stunned him. One day, Jesus approached his tax booth. No one knows exactly what Matthew was thinking as the Son of God stood before his table of coins—but it's not hard to imagine. Matthew had been chasing false refuges: wealth, power, the security of

Rome. But those things had left him empty. The money hadn't satisfied him. The empire hadn't protected him. In gaining the world, Matthew had lost himself—cut off from his people, far from God, and deeply alone.

And then Jesus showed up.

Jesus sees into the heart of every person—and He saw the pain in Matthew's. He knew the weight Matthew carried, the emptiness behind the wealth, the ache beneath the betrayal. And so, with divine tenderness, Jesus offered him a way out. He called Matthew to leave behind his false refuge and step into friendship with God. The coins that once seemed so valuable now meant nothing. They slipped from Matthew's hands and clattered onto the table—forgotten. In a single, life-changing sentence, the Gospel of Matthew captures this turning point in his life:

> As Jesus was walking along, he saw a man called Matthew sitting at the tax booth; and he said to him, "Follow me." And he got up and followed him. (Matthew 9:9)

Matthew looked up into the eyes of Christ—and without a word, he rose into a new life. In that silent moment, Matthew the Tax Collector became Matthew the Friend of God.

The story quickly shifts to a new scene. The tax booth was left behind for good, no longer part of Matthew's life. His conversion didn't lead to isolation or hesitation—it led to mission. Already, we see the beginnings of the evangelist he will become. Matthew brought Jesus straight into his home and filled it with the people he knew best. His house overflowed with tax collectors and other sinners. He wanted them all to meet the one who looked past his sin and called him by name. Matthew had encountered mercy—and now he wanted to share it.

Notice how quickly and naturally Matthew became comfortable with Jesus. There was no awkward distance, no hesitation. Matthew must have experienced Christ not just as a teacher or miracle-worker, but as a true friend—the kind of friend you invite into your home, the kind you introduce to the people closest to you.

Given the weight of Matthew's sin and betrayal, Jesus could have responded with sternness, as He sometimes did with the Pharisees. He could have spoken as a judge passing a sentence, declaring guilt and moving on. But He didn't. Jesus did not come to accuse—that's the work of the devil. He came to restore, to call us back into relationship. Yes, Jesus is the Judge. Yes, He is Lord. But wonderfully, mercifully—He is also our Friend.

As Jesus revealed the closeness of God to Matthew, the Pharisees who witnessed the event struggled to understand. They stood outside and wrung their hands. We read:

> As he sat at dinner in the house, many
> tax collectors and sinners came and were

> sitting with him and his disciples. When the Pharisees saw this, they said to his disciples, "Why does your teacher eat with tax collectors and sinners?" But when he heard this, he said, "Those who are well have no need of a physician, but those who are sick. Go and learn what this means, 'I desire mercy, not sacrifice.' For I have come to call not the righteous but sinners." (Matthew 9:10–13)

In this moment, Jesus revealed a secret of His heart: "I desire mercy."

But the Pharisees remained at a distance—physically and spiritually. They stood apart, watching from the false security of their self-righteousness. Their refusal to draw near to Jesus reflects an even deeper refusal to receive what He offers. While Christ extends the invitation to refuge, we must choose whether or not to accept it.

And here's something easy to overlook: Jesus genuinely *wanted* to be with Matthew and his friends. He delighted in their company. He sat at their table not out of obligation, but out of love. He longed to show them that God is not a distant taskmaster, but a loving Father—one in whom they could finally find true refuge. In the Gospel of John, when Jesus said to His disciples, "I have called you friends," He wasn't using poetic language. He meant it. As hard as it may be for us to grasp, Jesus truly wants to be our friend.

And in Matthew's home—amid the laughter, the

questions, the quiet wonder, and the grace—everyone gathered experienced something astonishing: the mind-blowing reality of being called a friend by Jesus—someone who knew them, welcomed them, and loved them in a way no one else ever had.

A Friend We Can Trust

Christ had a profound reason for becoming our Friend. As children of Adam and Eve, we carry a deep wound—a difficulty in trusting God. But through friendship, Jesus invites us to draw near without fear. He gives us space and time to become familiar with the Father's heart, to grow comfortable enough to step out from the shadows of our hiding places—the modern-day fig trees we cling to. I believe God delights in gently coaxing us out of the darkness and into the light of His love.

One of the great spiritual writers of our time, Fr. Jacques Philippe, captures this beautifully. In his short but powerful book *Searching for and Maintaining Peace*, he makes a surprising claim. The first goal of spiritual combat, he says, is not to eliminate every sin from our lives—not at first. The first goal is something deeper and more foundational: It is to trust in Jesus. He writes:

> The first goal of spiritual combat, that toward which our efforts must above all else be directed, is not to always obtain a victory (over our temptations,

our weaknesses, etc.), rather it is to learn to maintain peace of heart under all circumstances, even in the case of defeat. It is only in this way that we can pursue the other goal, which is the elimination of our failures, our faults, our imperfections and sins. This is ultimately the victory that we must want and desire, knowing, however, that it is not by our own strength that we will obtain it.[20]

Fr. Philippe points out that we often get things backward. Instead of trusting in God first and foremost, we place our trust in ourselves. We try to conquer our sins and fix our brokenness by our own strength, believing that once we've cleaned ourselves up, *then* we'll be worthy to come before God. But that's not how grace works. That's not the heart of the Gospel. As Fr. Philippe puts it:

> Quite often in the daily unfolding of our Christian life it happens that we fight the wrong battle, if one may put it that way, because we orient our efforts in the wrong direction. We fight on a terrain where the devil subtly drags us and can vanquish us, instead of

[20] Jacques Philippe, *Searching for and Maintaining Peace: A Small Treatise on Peace of Heart* (Alba House, 2002), 12.

> fighting on the real battlefield, where, on
> the contrary, by the grace of God, we are
> always certain of victory. And this is one
> of the great secrets of spiritual combat —
> to avoid fighting the wrong battle.[21]

Matthew had his experience of false refuge. His money did not fill his heart to overflowing; his money never loved him back. And perhaps because of this false refuge, Matthew understood the true refuge of Christ when he found it.

St. Augustine was another man who tasted the bitterness of false refuge. When he experienced Christ, Augustine tasted for the first time the fullness of life and peace of heart. He wrote: "Our hearts are restless until they rest in you."[22]

No matter what false refuge you've chased in life, the door back to Christ is always open. When we place our trust in the Friend of our soul, He welcomes us into His divine refuge. And it's there—in the stillness and peace of His presence—that true healing begins. That healing is the focus of our next chapter.

---

[21] Jacques Philippe, *Searching for and Maintaining Peace,* 11.
[22] *The Confessions of St. Augustine* (Image Books, 1960) Book I, Chapter I, 43.

Chapter 5

The Healer of Hearts

As for God, His way is perfect: The Lord's word is
flawless;
He shields all who take refuge in Him.
Psalm 18:30

A ll of us experience an anxious heart from
time to time. Left to ourselves in this fallen
world, we find ourselves longing—yearning—for
things the world simply cannot offer. We hunger
for everlasting life, but the world cannot give it.
We crave unshakable joy and peace, yet they remain just out of reach. These deepest desires of the
human heart can only be fulfilled by the healing

touch of Christ. And thanks be to God, this is exactly what the good Jesus desires for us. As He has said: "I came that they may have life, and have it abundantly" (John 10:10).

A few years ago, I traveled to another city to give a talk. That evening, after the event, I returned to my hotel room, looking forward to some rest before an early flight home.

As often happens when traveling, my usual routines were off. My wife and kids weren't with me, so instead of going through my familiar bedtime rituals, I opened my laptop and started watching *The Office*. It was something light and familiar—background noise, really. Partway through the episode, I opened another tab and began scrolling through the comments on one of my social media posts. Like so many of us today, I slipped into that digital double-dip—half-watching, half-scrolling.

The comments section on social media can be a dangerously distracting place; positive remarks from strangers compete with snide or hostile ones from other strangers. I waded into the mess, feeling myself getting a little worked up in the process. Then my phone buzzed—another distraction. A text message. With one hand still on the laptop, I started typing a reply on my iPhone with the other.

In less than ten minutes, I was engaged in three different activities. I was watching—well, at least listening to—*The Office* in one tab, scrolling through comments in another, and texting on my phone. I was mentally juggling a sitcom, a social feed, and a conversation—without really giving any of them my full attention.

Has that ever happened to you? I'm guessing it has.

These screens, these shows, this scrolling, these comments are all competing for our scattered attention. And the result? We don't feel rested. We feel drained. We go looking for peace, for a moment of quiet leisure, but we end up more tired, more anxious, and more irritable than before. The truth is, this isn't recreation or leisure at all; it's distraction. We often think we're winding down, but really, we're just numbing out. And there's a big difference between rest and distraction.

Let me explain.

Getting Rest versus Getting Distracted

Healthy recreation actually *re-creates* us. It renews us, restores us, and helps make us whole. The mental and physical restoration that comes from true rest is worlds apart from the draining, anxiety-inducing effects of dissociative activities. When we "zone out" through endless scrolling, passive screen time, or background noise, we're not becoming more ourselves—we're becoming less.

The Greek philosophers knew this. They identified a specific virtue for the art of resting well: *eutrapelia*. It refers to a healthy pleasantness, a kind of cheerful playfulness. It stands between two extremes—*boorishness*, the inability to relax, and *buffoonery*, the inability to take life seriously.

St. Thomas Aquinas took this idea and incorporated it into his own theology, recognizing *eutrapelia* as a part of the virtue of temperance. For Aquinas, it meant knowing how to rest rightly — striking the balance between too little and too much. Proper rest, for him, isn't about escape or indulgence. It's about restoration. It refreshes our energies so we can return to life renewed, not depleted.

St. Thomas wrote:

> Just as man needs bodily rest for the body's refreshment, . . . so too is it with his soul, whose power is also finite and equal to a fixed amount of work. Just as weariness of the body is dispelled by resting the body, so weariness of the soul is remedied by resting the soul: and the soul's rest is pleasure. Consequently, the remedy for weariness of soul must needs consist in the application of some pleasure, by slackening the tension of the reason's study.[23]

There in the hotel room, I wasn't practicing *eutrapelia*. I wasn't resting well — in fact, I wasn't resting at all. I was distracting myself in all the wrong ways. And instead of feeling restored, I felt

[23] St. Thomas Aquinas, *Summa Theologiae*, II–II, 168, 2.

more exhausted than when I started. I should have been relaxed, but I was agitated, frustrated, and mentally scattered.

What the Heart Needs

I share this story—and the forgotten virtue of *eutrapelia*—because it points us toward the one and only place of true rest: the refuge found in the heart of Christ. There, instead of being pulled apart, we are made whole. In contrast, the fallen world around us pulls us in countless directions and offers not rest but dissociation. These are not places of refuge—they are traps disguised as comfort.

St. Thomas Aquinas can help us here once again. In his writings, he observed that the world offers us many things that *promise* happiness: wealth, fame, honor, power, pleasure, the goods of the body, the goods of the soul, and all created things.[24]

These things can be good—but they cannot fulfill us. Aquinas shows how each one ultimately falls short. None of them can satisfy the deep longing of the human heart, because we weren't made for passing pleasures or temporary comforts. We were made for something far greater: unveiled and uninterrupted communion with God. And that perfect happiness—*complete and lasting beatitude*—can never be fully had in this life. It awaits us in Heaven.

But even now, in this life, we're not left empty-handed. We're given glimpses—foretastes—of that

---

[24] See *Summa Theologiae*, I–II, 2.

eternal joy. When we entrust ourselves to God and rest in His love, something within us settles. The scattered heart is gathered. The weary soul finds peace. Not perfectly, not yet—but real. These restoring experiences remind us where our true home lies—heaven.

When I was around sixteen or seventeen, I was out on the town with some friends in Adelaide. We'd spent the whole night partying—too much to drink, too much noise, chasing the kind of thrill we all assumed would make us happy. As dawn approached, we wandered through the quiet streets of the city, still laughing, still buzzing from the night.

That's when I noticed it. The sun was beginning to rise over the skyline. Its light spread slowly and steadily, illuminating everything with a kind of quiet majesty. And as it did, the neon signs that had lit up the night—those glowing blues and reds advertising clubs and bars—started to fade. Started to lose their charm. Against the brilliance of the sunrise, they looked weak, sad, almost embarrassed to still be shining. Their glow couldn't compete with the sunrise.

That image has stayed with me. Because what the sunrise was to those neon lights, Christ is to the false pleasures of the world. When He begins to dawn in our hearts, the things that once dazzled us begin to lose their grip. Their appeal fades—not because we've gritted our teeth and repressed our desires, but because we've finally found something greater to direct them toward. The human heart was made for light, not for flickering imitations.

I want to turn now to Scripture and meditate on

a passage that reveals Christ as the healer of our hearts.

Reaching for Jesus

There is a beautiful story in the Gospels—an encounter between Jesus and a woman who had suffered for many years. We read:

> There was a woman who had had a discharge of blood for twelve years, and who had suffered much under many physicians, and had spent all that she had, and was no better but rather grew worse. (Mark 5:25–27)

This poor, forgotten woman was physically weak, financially ruined, and spiritually exhausted because of her relentless illness. For many years she had gone from doctor to doctor, treatment to treatment, pouring out her money and hope in equal measure—only to be left worse off than before.

Each time she met a new physician, her heart would rise with fragile hope. Maybe this one could help. She would pay the fee, follow the treatment, cling to the possibility of healing—and wait. Sometimes, for a brief moment, it would feel like something had improved. Yet, despite everything, the illness endured, dragging her into deeper pain and disillusionment. She was getting worn out by a hope that only ever led to heartbreak. Thus, for twelve exhausting years, she had been trapped in a relentless cycle of emotional highs and lows.

Then one day, Jesus passed through her town. The rumors of His healing power had already spread. And though her heart warned her not to hope again—not to risk another disappointment—something within her stirred. She couldn't resist Him. She felt drawn to Christ. Quietly, almost secretly, she decided to approach Him, saying to herself, "If I touch even his garments, I will be made well" (Mark 5:28).

This simple act was a profound expression of faith. In reaching for His garment, she was reaching past human remedies and abandoning herself to the only true refuge left: Jesus Himself. It was a moment of surrender—not to despair, but to divine mercy.

With trembling hands, she pushed through the crowd. Her eyes stayed fixed on Him as she drew closer, step by step, until she stood just behind Him. Then, gently, she reached out and touched the edge of His cloak. And all along, Jesus knew what was happening.

In His usual awesome way, Christ perceived everything. He sees each person. Every heart. Every wound. Every silent prayer. Every hidden desire. Nothing escapes Him.

Of course He understood this woman's pain. He knew her fears, her shame, her sense of unworthiness. He knew that she couldn't bring herself to stand before Him face-to-face. Her suffering had shaped her—taught her to shrink back, remain unseen. And so she came to Him in the only way she knew how: quietly, from behind.

And He let her.

> Immediately the flow of blood dried up, and she felt in her body that she was healed of her disease. And Jesus, perceiving in himself that power had gone out from him, immediately turned about in the crowd and said, "Who touched my garments?" (Mark 5:29–30)

This is the tender genius of Christ. The compassionate heart of Jesus welcomes even the most hesitant act of faith. He adapts Himself to the condition of each soul. He stoops—not out of pity, but out of perfect love. In this moment, it was as though He turned His back to her—not to distance Himself, but to draw her in. What looked like Him turning away was, in fact, His way of coming closer. He met her exactly where she was so He could lift her to where she was meant to be. Jesus said to her, "Daughter, your faith has made you well; go in peace, and be healed of your disease" (Mark 5:33–34).

With these simple words, Christ revealed to her the true nature of God. He shattered, once and for all, the image of a distant or vengeful deity who inflicts illness and hardship as punishment. Instead, He looked at her and called her *daughter*.

Christ shattered the darkness of her existence in a way that defied all cultural and societal expectations of the time. Her Jewish faith, as it was commonly understood then, taught that illness was a consequence of sin. So she lived not only with pain but also with guilt. In her eyes, her affliction wasn't just unfortunate—it was deserved, a punishment. This belief slowly ate away at her dignity. She couldn't see herself as a beloved daughter of God. The idea that God's love might actually extend to *her* was unthinkable. If you had asked her whether God loved her, she likely would've said no. Not someone like her. God, she believed, loved the holy people—the ones who were clean, worthy, devout. But her? She was too far gone. Too broken. Too unclean.

Thankfully, on that day, everything changed. Her encounter with Christ transformed not only her body but also her soul. She placed her hope in Him—and was healed. But Jesus didn't let the moment end there. He called her forward, inviting her to step out of the shadows and publicly acknowledge Him. In doing so, He gave her the opportunity to rise above her doubts, her fear, and the shame that had defined her for so long.

This wasn't just a personal healing—it was a public restoration. The crowd, who likely knew her story, who had perhaps whispered and judged her as someone marked by sin, witnessed something extraordinary. Christ didn't just heal her—He honored her. He lifted her up in front of them all, unveiling the beauty of a soul that had dared to trust in God. And in doing so,

He taught everyone watching a profound lesson: while they may have seen a woman cursed and cast aside, God saw a woman of great faith—blessed, restored, and beloved.

In that moment, everything changed. Her heart awakened to the profound truth at the center of all faith: God is a loving Father.

The word *daughter* was the most beautiful thing she had ever heard. Just as her body had been healed by touching Christ, her heart and soul were healed by hearing His voice. That single word restored her dignity, her identity, her place in God's family. And in the end, that inner healing—the healing of her spirit—was even more miraculous than the physical cure.

Seek Healing!

The woman with the hemorrhage never stopped longing to be made whole. Her suffering was always before her; she couldn't forget it. But more importantly, she never gave up the desire to be healed. She didn't settle. We can learn a lot from her witness. When we're weighed down by sin, we often find ourselves afraid of God and reluctant to trust Him. That's unfortunate—because Christ has revealed the exact opposite of what we fear. He's shown us that we can approach our Father and rest under His loving gaze. This is what God wills.

If there is anyone in the universe we should feel safe and at peace with, it is our heavenly Father.

He knows everything about us—every failure, every fear, every wound—and still, He cherishes us. His name is Mercy. We can trust Him.

But our lack of trust doesn't come from nowhere. Some of it, quite frankly, needs to be laid at the devil's doorstep. Just as he deceived Adam and Eve in the garden, the enemy still whispers the same lie: God is not to be trusted. He's holding something back. He's disappointed in us, or worse, disgusted by us. These lies stir up an unholy fear that drives us further from God, right into despair. The devil knows that a heart divided is a heart he can control.

We see his fingerprints all over one of the most insidious lies of our time: *You are fine just the way you are*. It sounds like an affirmation, but it's a trap. If we believe we're already fine—no change needed, no healing required—then we'll never reach out for the hem of Christ's garment. We'll stay in our wounds, convincing ourselves they're not wounds at all.

Our culture repeats this lie in a thousand subtle ways—but let's be honest: We aren't fine just the way we are. We have real problems. We're wounded, disordered, and often far from where we should be. We always need healing. We always need transformation. And these only come when we're willing to cooperate with God's grace—when we admit our need, humble ourselves, and begin the journey of change. Without that willingness, we remain stuck—and in danger.

The woman with the hemorrhage never said to herself, "This is just who I am. I'm fine this way." Her honesty and humility prepared her to seek and receive the healing Christ offered. By contrast, the Pharisees represent those who *don't* receive healing—because they don't think they need it. Their pride blinded them. Their sense of self-sufficiency closed them off from grace. They couldn't be healed because they wouldn't admit they were sick.

We see this tension reach a dramatic peak in John's Gospel. Jesus entered the Temple during Hanukkah—the Feast of Dedication. A crowd gathered around Him, intrigued. There was growing curiosity, even excitement. Some were beginning to wonder: *Could this really be the Messiah?* And so, with anticipation hanging in the air, they asked Him: "How long will you keep us in suspense? If you are the Messiah, tell us plainly" (John 10:25).

Jesus' answer was very clear, but not in the way they expected. He ended His response to them by saying: "The Father and I are one" (John 10:30).

Jesus' statement implied equality with God, an idea that sounded blasphemous to pious Jewish ears. These Jews who had learned from Jesus, who had been inclined to believe in Him, instead turned against Him. They pivoted from pious Jews to an enraged mob. The Gospel of John says: "The Jews took up stones again to stone him" (John 10:31).

These Jews didn't see themselves as sick, so they didn't seek healing. They didn't think they needed saving, so the offer of salvation sounded not only unnecessary—it sounded offensive. The gift of eternal life, the invitation to be healed and made whole, struck them as unreasonable. And instead of reaching out their broken hands to touch the hem of His garment, they reached for stones.

We may never hurl stones at Christ with our hands, but we often do so with our lives. Every time we cling to sin, every time we reject His grace, we wound Him again. Every sin adds to the weight of His suffering. Every act of rebellion drives the nails deeper. As Scripture says, when we sin deliberately, we are "crucifying once again the Son of God" (Hebrews 6:6).

But there is another way—the way of trust and return. Jesus is the one and only refuge for the human soul. In His arms, we find healing. In His heart, we find peace. We must turn back to Him.

The next section of this book is about that return. It's the journey back to the Father's house. It's the invitation God extends to every soul. And often, it begins in the most unlikely of places—in the filth and sorrow of the pigsty, when we finally awaken to the gravity of our sin and remember where we truly belong.

Part II
The Path to Refuge

Chapter 6

Trapped in False Refuge

They served their idols, which became a snare to them. They sacrificed their sons and their daughters to demons.
Psalm 106:36–37

And they abandoned the Lord, the God of their fathers, who had brought them out of the land of Egypt. They went after other gods, from among the gods of the peoples who were around them, and bowed down to them.
Judges 2:12

C hrist is our one true and eternal refuge. And yet, despite this beautiful reality, we're still drawn to seek shelter elsewhere. We run to alcohol, money, drugs, toxic relationships—false havens that promise relief but deliver ruin. These aren't places of rest; they're traps dressed up as escape hatches. It reminds me of the old story of Hansel and Gretel from *Grimm's Fairy Tales*. You remember that one, don't you? Despite it being a tale often read to children, I think it might be one of the most disturbing and frightening stories I've ever read—and one of my favorites. In it, two children—Hansel and Gretel—are cruelly mistreated, not once, but twice, by two wicked women.

The first woman is their wicked stepmother. She persuades the children's father to abandon them in the woods to die. Her reasoning? A famine has struck the land, and there isn't enough food to feed all four of them. If the children are gone, she argues, at least the two of them will survive. Tragically—and with tragic cowardice—their father agrees. And so Hansel and Gretel are led deep into the forest and left to fend for themselves, alone and in danger.

Naturally, the children search for a place of refuge. And this is where the second evil woman enters the story. Deep in the woods, a witch has built a house entirely out of edible sweets. The famished children stumble upon it and, without hesitation, run to it, eager to satisfy their hunger. They ask no questions; they just indulge. But as they're feasting, the witch steps out and invites them inside with the promise of even more. What began as a dream turns into a nightmare. Once through the door, they become prisoners. Hansel is locked up and fattened like livestock for slaughter. Gretel is forced into servitude, made to wait on the witch like a household slave.

Thankfully, Gretel outsmarts the witch, shoving her into the oven and ending the nightmare. The siblings escape, their pockets full of treasure and their lives intact.

Hansel and Gretel ran toward something that looked good on the outside—a house made of sweets, a dream come true for starving children. But it was a trap, a pseudo-refuge, shiny on the surface but rotten at the core. It's the kind of tale many parents shy away from at bedtime—when, in my estimation, it's precisely the kind of story we *should* be reading to our children. It speaks to something real and hauntingly familiar: the nature of the world, the evils our kids will have to confront, and the trials they'll one day be called to overcome.

In this fallen world, traps are everywhere—cleverly disguised and dressed in appealing slogans. One real example? "Life is short. Have an affair."[25] God have mercy! These lies promise beauty, comfort, escape. They offer to fix us, fulfill us, perfect our lives. But it's all a lie.

Many people believe these lies. They flock to false places of refuge in search of comfort or escape—Pornhub, alcohol, Tinder, Uber Eats, social media, drugs, and the like. Now, not all of these are bad in and of themselves (Uber Eats, for

---

[25] The original tagline to the Ashley Madison website promoting adultery.

example, can be a gift on a busy night). But when we turn to them to console ourselves, to numb our pain, or to avoid facing ourselves, they become something else entirely. Some bring a sense of guilt and remorse. Others try to muffle our conscience with a stream of justifications. And over time, these counterfeit refuges begin to take on a religious shape. They become our gods.

The shock of that reality becomes clearer if we reimagine just one biblical verse, substituting one of these false gods in place of the true God. Here's Psalm 18:2 with one such substitution: *Pornhub is my rock, my fortress, and my deliverer; my God is Pornhub, in whom I take refuge.*

Looking for Happiness

One night, after we'd put the kids to bed, my wife, Cameron, was on the couch reading a book, and I was rummaging through the pantry, trying to satisfy one of those vague, late-night cravings. I didn't know what I wanted—just that I was hungry for something. I moved aside cookies, chips, leftover Easter candy, granola bars . . . nothing was quite right. After a few minutes, Cameron looked up and asked, "What are you looking for?"

I paused and half-jokingly said, "I'm looking for happiness."

We all do this, don't we? We all want happiness, but we don't always know where to find it, or even what exactly we're looking for. And when that search turns away from God, the doorway to sin quietly opens. Sin doesn't usually begin with something obviously evil. More often, it starts small—a minor misstep, a seemingly harmless choice—that gradually leads us down a path far from the Father.

It might begin with a quick decision about something trivial, which sets off a chain of choices with heavier consequences. Like the gambler who buys a cheap lottery ticket, then ups the stakes after a loss, hoping to win it all back. Or the person who answers a message from someone they shouldn't be communicating with. Or maybe it's something subtler—choosing a real good, but at the expense of a greater one. Like filling a rare free moment with social media instead of spending it with your children.

The Lies We Tell Ourselves

When we seek refuge anywhere other than God, it's often after we've convinced ourselves we have good reasons for doing so. Scripture reveals that this tendency isn't new. In fact, the Bible presents at least five different attitudes we can adopt when turning away from God as our refuge.

Denial

One common attitude is to convince ourselves that the false refuge is actually helping us. We see this in the Parable of the Prodigal Son. After leaving his father's house, the son travels to a distant land and eventually hits rock bottom—working in a pigsty, starving, and desperate. For a faithful Jew, tending to unclean animals like pigs would have been deeply humiliating—ritually and personally degrading. And yet that's where the prodigal son ends up. Luke tells us, "He would gladly have filled himself with the pods that the pigs were eating" (Luke 15:16). He's not just near the pigs—he envies them for the husks they were eating. That's how far he's fallen. And still, for a time, he clings to that false refuge, as though it might eventually satisfy.

When St. Augustine and St. Bede reflected on this passage centuries ago, what stood out to them was the nature of the husks themselves. They weren't real food. They offered no nourishment—only the illusion of it. St. Bede wrote: "The husk is a sort of bean, empty within, soft outside, by which the body is not refreshed, but filled, so that it rather loads than nourishes."[26]

St. Augustine builds on this idea with a moral interpretation. For him, the empty husks represent the vanities of the world—things that promise fulfillment but leave the soul empty. They fill, but they do not nourish. He writes: "The husks are the doctrines of the world: they swell the belly, but they do not nourish the soul." It's a sobering image—one that captures the deceptive nature of sin and the hollowness of all the things we chase apart from God.

St. Augustine continues: "The husks then with

---

[26] St Thomas Aquinas, *Catena Aurea*, Vol III. C. 15.

which the swine were fed are the teaching of the world, which cries loudly of vanity; according to which in various prose and verse men repeat the praises of the idols, and fables belonging to the gods of the Gentiles, wherewith the devils are delighted."[27]

Eating the husks was never going to nourish him, but the prodigal son was inclined to believe they might. Yet even in his desperation, *no one gave him anything*. It's a picture of utter emptiness—craving, deception, and rejection all at once. And we're not so different. We can deny that something in our life is harming us. Like the prodigal son, who believed joy was waiting somewhere beyond the father's house, we too can go far from home—in denial that what we've chosen is quietly undoing us.

Presumption

Another attitude we often adopt is presumption. We believe our false refuge is not that dangerous, or if we recognize the danger, that we're strong enough to handle it. This mindset shows up clearly in the life of Lot in the Book of Genesis.

Lot was Abraham's nephew, the son of Abraham's brother Haran. After Haran's death, Lot journeyed with Abraham (then still called Abram) toward the land of Canaan. In time, both men had acquired so many herds and possessions that the land could no longer support their living side by side. So they

---

[27] *Catena Aurea*, Vol III. C. 15.

decided to part ways. Abraham, showing great generosity, gave Lot the first choice of where to settle. He said to him: "If you take the left hand, then I will go to the right; or if you take the right hand, then I will go to the left" (Genesis 13:9).

Lot could have settled his family in any number of places—but he chose the fertile plains near Sodom, drawn by the promise of prosperity and security. In doing so, he turned a blind eye to the wickedness of the people who lived there. He ignored what should have alarmed him, allowing comfort and sin to coexist in his life. That choice would come at a great cost. By making a home near Sodom, Lot exposed his family to the corruption of that city—corruption that would eventually lead to their devastation and near ruin (see Genesis 19).

Like Lot, we can easily shove moral dangers into some forgotten corner of our lives. We make peace with certain sins, convincing ourselves they're not a big deal. But they don't stay quiet forever. Sooner or later, like a pebble in the shoe, a snowball gathering speed, or a spark in a dry forest, our compromise catches up with us. What we presumed was small becomes something we can't ignore.

Defiance

Some adopt an attitude of outright defiance toward God. They construct for themselves a rival refuge—a counterfeit stronghold meant to contend with the true one. This pattern shows up early in salvation history. In the Book of Genesis, we see it clearly in the stories of Cain and the Tower of Babel.

After Cain killed his brother Abel and was driven into exile, we're told:

> Cain went away from the presence of the Lord, and settled in the land of Nod, east of Eden. Cain knew his wife, and she conceived and bore Enoch; and he built a city, and named it Enoch. (Genesis 4:16–17)

Cain's first act after leaving the presence of God—a separation that foreshadows the pattern of sin—was to build a city. Perhaps he was seeking safety, identity, and control apart from God. He convinced himself that a man-made refuge could give him what he needed. But the city couldn't erase his guilt or undo the curse he bore.

Later, after the flood in Noah's time, humanity once again banded together in defiance. They began building the Tower of Babel, determined to reach the heavens. They told themselves they would never be destroyed by a flood again—despite the visible promise of God's mercy in the rainbow. They placed their trust not in God, but in their own strength.

Like Cain and the men of Babel, we too can resent God's Lordship and try to carve out our own refuge. Sin inclines us to rely on ourselves, to build walls instead of altars. But every man-made refuge eventually fails. Unless we turn to Christ's refuge, our defiance will only end in disaster.

Self-Reliance

Another attitude we often take is more subtle. It's not outright defiance—it's self-reliance dressed up as prudence. We convince ourselves that the false refuge we've built is "good enough" and we don't really need anything more. We're not rebelling against God, exactly; we're just "doing it our way" because it feels safer. Because we love control.

This attitude comes to life in the Parable of the Rich Fool from Luke's Gospel:

> The land of a rich man produced abundantly. And he thought to himself, 'What should I do, for I have no place to store my crops?' Then he said, 'I will do this: I will pull down my barns and build larger ones, and there I will store all my grain and my goods. And I will say to my soul, Soul, you have ample goods laid up for many years; relax, eat, drink, be merry.' But God said to him, 'You fool! This very night your life is being demanded of you. And the things you have prepared, whose will they be?' So it is with those who store up

treasures for themselves but are not
rich toward God. (Luke 12:16–21)

This man tried to turn his wealth into a refuge.
You can almost hear the strain in his voice as he
tries to convince himself: "I will say to my soul . . .
I will say to my soul . . ." If he repeated it enough,
it's as if he might finally believe it. But deep down,
he knew it wasn't true. And then came the voice of
God: "You fool!"

Like him, we try to talk ourselves out of fear and
into peace. We attempt to self-soothe with possessions, routines, or achievements. We feel hopeful
when our finances are strong, and we despair
when they're not. But peace built on a foundation
of self-reliance will always crack under pressure.
True security comes only from being rich toward
God.

Lack of Complete Trust

Lastly, similar to self-reliance, there's another
common attitude, which is to *appear* trusting in
God, all the while secretly keeping a backup plan.
We say we rely on Him, but in reality we hedge our
bets. We want to be faithful, but we also want a
safety net we can control.

This kind of half-trust is embodied in the story of
King Saul. He didn't fully carry out God's command
to destroy the Amalekites, choosing instead to follow
his own reasoning. At first glance, his disobedience

may seem minor—but this seemingly small act revealed a deeper issue: Saul trusted himself more than he trusted God.

Later, facing a massive Philistine army, Saul was overcome with fear: "When Saul saw the army of the Philistines, he was afraid, and his heart trembled greatly" (1 Samuel 28:5).

Instead of turning to God in repentance or trust, Saul sought a different refuge. He went to a medium—the witch of Endor—to try and gain secret knowledge about the future. In doing so, he not only disobeyed God again but directly violated His law. Saul wanted the comfort of certainty, even if it meant turning to forbidden means.

But this false refuge gave him no peace. The message he received didn't deliver him—it only confirmed his doom. The refuge he reached for was empty, because it was not God. Every time we lack trust in God and instead trust in ourselves, we rob ourselves of the very stability we hope to find.

The Way Out

All of these attitudes we adopt toward false refuges—whether open defiance, quiet self-reliance, or half-hearted trust—lead us to the same place: suffering and sin. They are dead ends, hollow spaces devoid of life. And yet, we keep going back to them.

I hope we can all hear the blunt but beautiful question asked by the angel on Easter morning:

"Why do you look for the living among the dead? He is not here, but has risen" (Luke 24:5).

We return to these false refuges for many reasons—to feel safe, to self-soothe, to numb the emotional turbulence we don't quite know how to handle. When we feel rejected, unloved, overlooked, or criticized, we often reach instinctively for the things we've trained ourselves to turn to—those false comforts we've relied on before.

But the first step toward healing is honesty. We need to name the false refuges in our lives. Ask yourself:

- What unhealthy places do I run to when I feel anxious or wounded?
- What toxic people or patterns do I keep returning to?
- What habits or pleasures do I use to escape discomfort?

When we name our false refuges—when we admit we've forsaken Christ, our true refuge, for lesser things—we can finally turn back to the Father. And when we do, we won't find condemnation. We'll find open arms.

Take a moment to quiet your heart and pray:

> *Good Father, I thank You. Thank you for loving me—not in some distant, obligatory sense, but personally. You like me. You delight in me. I know You desire my*

holiness and that You are bringing it about in Your own perfect time. You, Father, are my refuge and my strength. I do not want the false refuges of this world. I want You.

And then, in the quiet of your heart, listen. I pray you can hear these words of Jesus—so tender, so true—like a balm for the soul:

Come to me, all you who labor and are heavy laden, and I will give you rest. (Matthew 11:28)

Fear not, little flock, for it hath pleased your Father to give you a kingdom. (Luke 12:32, DRA).

Chapter 7

The True Weight of Sin

For the wages of sin is death, but the free gift
of God is eternal life in Christ Jesus our Lord.
Romans 6:23

Sin, when it is fully grown, gives birth to death.
James 1:15

A distinctly postmodern habit many of us fall into—often without realizing it—is the emptying of language of its true meaning. We abuse speech by dressing up grave realities in euphemisms that dull the moral weight of what's being said. The mutilation of a child's body becomes "gender-affirming care." Adultery, once understood as a serious betrayal, is now casually dismissed as "cheating," as if it were just breaking the rules of a board game. And words like *fornication* and *abortion* are rebranded as *sleeping together* and *essential women's healthcare*, lest we sound too harsh or judgmental.

Along the same lines, we tend to avoid speaking plainly about personal sin. Instead, we call sins *mistakes* or say we "messed up." We prefer to focus on our weakness, brokenness, past wounds, and trauma. By softening the language, we make it easier to shift blame outward—and harder to take responsibility. The result? No real call to conversion. Even some of the Church's most powerful truths, like divine mercy, are not immune to this erosion of meaning. In his book *Conversion*, Fr. Donald Haggerty highlights several modern spiritual confusions—one of which is our distorted understanding of mercy itself. He writes:

> Among the spiritual confusions of the current day, unfortunately, a misunderstanding of divine mercy is high on the list. For many people, God's mercy has shifted from divine forgiveness offered to the repentant sinner to a divine pity for the sinner who persists in sin and seems unable to extricate himself from his sin. In this understanding, mercy is directed primarily, not at the forgiveness of particular sins, but at the painful sense of guilt for sin. The sin itself is a secondary consideration, while mercy is somewhat

like a spiritual blanket covering the soul with the warmth of divine compassion. Receiving mercy in this view does not at all require a struggle to overcome sin. Instead, it has become akin to an act of amnesty, a divine reprieve granted to a guilty conscience. It simply releases a soul from the burden of shame felt after committing sin.[28]

Today, spiritual confusion abounds—one of the most dangerous being our tendency to whitewash sin and downplay its seriousness. Yet *sin*, as uncomfortable as the word may be, must remain in our moral vocabulary with all its weight and ugliness intact. If we lose the language for evil, we lose our ability to recognize it. As the prophet Isaiah warned:

> Woe to those who call evil good and good evil, who put darkness for light and light for darkness, who put bitter for sweet and sweet for bitter!
> (Isaiah 5:20)

The New Atheist's False Refuge

Forgetting about sin has real consequences. In the early 2000s, a wave of atheists rose to prominence by

---

[28] Fr. Donald Haggerty, *Conversion: Spiritual Insights into an Essential Encounter with God* (Ignatius Press, 2017), 75.

launching aggressive attacks on religion. Their books filled airport kiosks and bookstore shelves, earning the movement the name "New Atheism." One of its most well-known voices, Christopher Hitchens, published *God Is Not Great: How Religion Poisons Everything* — a title that leaves little doubt about his views. Though the intellectual caliber of these writers falls short of earlier atheists like Nietzsche or Sartre, their message struck a cultural nerve and left a lasting mark.

The New Atheists were offering yet another false refuge — this time in reason and science. Their basic claim was simple: The world would be better off without religion. If humanity could finally dock in the safe harbor of reason over faith and science over Scripture, we'd usher in a brighter, more moral future. Religious belief, they argued, had done more harm than good; only a reasoned, god-less morality could save us. In their view, utopia begins where God ends.

The bold claims of the New Atheists have proven not only false but devastating. Their project has failed. As St. John Paul II wisely wrote in *Fides et Ratio*, "Faith and reason are like two wings on which the human spirit rises to the contemplation of truth."[29] But when a culture tries to soar with only one wing — reason severed from faith — it doesn't rise; it plummets. And so it has.

To be clear, the New Atheists didn't cause this

---

[29] John Paul II, *Fides et Ratio* (September 1998), 1.

collapse on their own, but they certainly helped accelerate it. Their rejection of religion gave a kind of intellectual permission for society to do the same—and soon we found ourselves in the wreckage of reason. A world where men can be pregnant, children can change sexes, and marriage can mean anything at all didn't emerge in a vacuum.

This wreckage has a cause: sin. And it's vital we understand what that means. Many Christians—Catholics and Protestants alike—have adopted a watered-down view of sin. We've grown too comfortable with it, too casual about its consequences.

So let's talk about sin.

Sin's Origin Story

Long before the rise of Christianity, the Greeks, Romans, and Jews had each developed some understanding of sin.

In Greek culture, the main word for what we now call "sin" was *hamartia*—literally meaning "to miss the mark," like an archer failing to hit a target. As Greek thought matured, *hamartia* took on deeper moral significance. It came to describe not just an error, but a tragic flaw in character—often pride or poor judgment—that leads to a person's downfall. A classic example is Icarus, whose reckless overconfidence drove him to fly too close to the sun, melting his wax wings and plunging him to his death.

The Romans had their own word for sin:

peccatum, which means "to stumble." Like the Greek *hamartia*, *peccatum* eventually carried moral weight. But the Roman view of sin was often tied more closely to civic and social obligations. A Roman citizen was expected to fulfill duties to the gods, the family, and the state. Failing in these responsibilities—whether through cowardice, dishonor, or neglecting religious rites—was considered a kind of moral failing, not just personally but socially.

Alongside these ancient Western civilizations, the Chosen People—the Israelites—had a unique and divinely guided understanding of sin. Unlike the Greeks and Romans, their view wasn't shaped merely by reason or cultural reflection, but by revelation. They didn't begin with abstract theories about sin; they began with God revealing its origin. In the Book of Genesis, they learned that sin has a cosmic weight. Adam and Eve's original act of disobedience wounded all of creation and introduced a fallen state that gave rise to every future sin. From that moment on, the people of Israel experienced sin not only as personal failure but as collective covenant-breaking. Again and again, they turned from God, and again and again, they bore the consequences.

Christianity inherited the rich cultural patrimony of the Greeks and Romans, along with the revealed Hebrew Scriptures. Drawing from these earlier understandings of sin—and guided by the light of the New Testament—Christianity was uniquely positioned to grasp the full depth and seriousness of sin.

Two key novelties stand out in the Christian understanding:

> 1. While the Greek word *hamartia* meant "missing the mark," Christianity clarified what that mark actually is: the glory of God. As St. Paul writes, "All have sinned and fall short of the glory of God" (Romans 3:23). Sin, then, is not merely a personal flaw or moral misstep—it is a personal offense against God, a failure to live in right relationship with Him. More than just an ethical error, sin carries eternal weight; it has eschatological consequences. Christians came to see that sin matters ultimately because it can jeopardize our salvation.

> 2. While the Book of Genesis offers profound insight into the origin of sin—what we now call *original* sin—it is in Christianity that this revelation finds its fulfillment. Like followers of Judaism, Christians recognize that sin has become part of the universal human condition: All are born into it, and all are wounded by it. But whereas the Old Testament looked forward in hope to a future remedy, the New Testament reveals that remedy in full. In the Gospels, we encounter not just a diagnosis of the problem,

but the definitive cure. The way out of sin is the Paschal Mystery—the Passion, death, and Resurrection of Jesus Christ. Christianity proclaims, with urgency and clarity, that Christ's offer of salvation is the one and only true refuge from sin.

Christ made it unmistakably clear that He alone is our refuge: "I am the way, and the truth, and the life. No one comes to the Father except through me" (John 14:6).

The refuge Christ offers is a place of mercy. Just a century ago, in Poland, St. Faustina Kowalska was given extraordinary revelations from Jesus about the depth of God's mercy. In her diary, she recorded many of these consoling words. Here is one such message from the Lord to Faustina:

In the Old Covenant I sent prophets wielding thunderbolts to My People. Today I am sending you with My mercy to the people of the whole world. I do not want to punish aching mankind, but I desire to heal it, pressing it to My Merciful Heart.[30]

When speaking about sin, the *Catechism* echoes the words of St. Paul: "Where sin increased, grace

---

[30] *Diary of Saint Maria Faustina Kowalska* (*Marian Press*, 2010), 1588.

abounded all the more" (Romans 5:20). But it also offers a crucial clarification—God's mercy cannot heal what we refuse to acknowledge. "Grace must uncover sin so as to convert our hearts" (*CCC*, 1848). In a culture that either misunderstands sin or refuses to name it altogether, this uncovering becomes all the more difficult—yet all the more necessary.

Two Common Approaches to Sin Today

Ask a handful of Christians from the pews to describe the nature of sin, and you'll likely get a range of answers. These responses generally fall into three categories, shaped largely by the church they attend and the voices they hear from the pulpit.

The first view stems from thinking *too little* of sin. This mindset tends to take root in communities that avoid speaking about sin, hell, or the devil. To be fair, their intention is often noble: They seek a faith that is Christ-centered, not sin-centered. The focus is rightly on the victory of Jesus, not the schemes of the enemy. And yes—God has won. The devil is a defeated, cowardly wretch who barks louder than he bites.

But while the war is won, the battle rages on. Until we reach heaven, we're still in the fight. And it's spiritually negligent to send people into that battle unequipped. When sin is downplayed or ignored, believers are left vulnerable. They may forget that real damage can still be done to their souls. Thinking too little of sin doesn't just distort the Gospel—it weakens our resistance to evil.

The danger of thinking too little about sin is that we begin to imagine that God simply winks at our "mistakes"—as if He were a gentle grandfather who pats us on the head but never calls us higher. In this view, divine love becomes indulgent rather than transformative.

This mindset often leads to the *psychologizing* of sin. Rather than taking responsibility, we deflect— pointing to our brokenness, woundedness, or past traumas. And while these are real and do shape us, they do not erase our free will. We are still moral agents, capable of choosing the good. Embracing a permanent posture of victimhood may feel comforting, but it ultimately paralyzes the soul.

When sin is treated as something trivial—a slip, a quirk, no worse than rolling through a stop sign or forgetting to say "please"—we lose sight of its seriousness. If God's commandments are reduced to arbitrary rules, our violations become justifiable, even forgettable. But sin is not a minor infraction. It is a rupture in our relationship with God.

A second way people often misunderstand sin is by being *too practical* about it—treating it as a mere contractual debt to be repaid. In this view, sin becomes less a rupture in a relationship and more a line item on a spiritual ledger. The deeply personal nature of sin—its offense against a loving God—is lost.

Many well-meaning, law-abiding people live in a world of financial transactions: loans, payments, interest, deadlines. It's easy, then, to project this mindset onto our spiritual lives. Sin becomes something we "owe," and confession becomes the routine payment. We mentally check off items on a list: *Did I swear? Skip Mass? Look at something I shouldn't have?* Once confessed, the "debt" is cleared—until the next cycle begins.

The danger here is subtle but serious. This mindset allows sin to become a normalized part of life, something we live with rather than fight against. Because we think our sins "hurt no one," we fail to grasp their true malice. But sin always wounds—ourselves, others, and most of all, our relationship with God. When sin becomes routine, so does spiritual stagnation. Growth becomes impossible where sin is comfortably tolerated.

An Honest Approach: Keeping Sin Real

The third—and truest—way to understand sin is through the lens of the Gospel. This means keeping Christ's Passion and death always before us. Sin is what led Him to the Cross—not just sin in general, but *my* sin and *your* sin. To be clear, sin is not the center of our faith—Christ is. But it was because of sin that Jesus came. He took on flesh to conquer it, to heal what we had broken, and to restore us to the Father.

Fr. Robert Hugh Benson, a Catholic priest who

converted from Anglicanism and was the son of an archbishop of Canterbury, gives us a powerful image of sin in his book *The Friendship of Christ*. He writes:

> Look at the crucifix. Then turn and look at the Sinner. Both are, in themselves, repulsive and horrible . . .: both are lovely and desirable, since Christ is in both: both are infinitely pathetic and appealing, since in both He "that knew no sin" is "made sin" (2 Corinthians 5:21). For the crucifix and the Sinner are profoundly, and not merely superficially, alike in this—that both are what the rebellious self-will of man has made of the Image of God.[31]

Christ died for our sins. We cannot speak this truth without also acknowledging its personal weight: *My sins*—past, present, and future—contributed to the crucifixion of Our Lord. This is why Fr. Robert Hugh Benson can say that a person mired in serious sin is, in a sense, a walking crucifix—carrying the marks of rebellion that Christ bore out of love.

When we perceive sin's reality, we begin to grasp its full dimension. Outwardly, sin is a rebellion against God—a betrayal of His love. Inwardly, it is a corrosive force that tears apart our lives, our

---

[31] Robert Hugh Benson, *The Friendship of Christ* (Longmans, Green, and Co., 1912), 91.

families, and our souls. Sin is not a minor misstep or a breach of arbitrary rules. It reaches into the very core of who we are, what we love, and how we live. Until we see sin in this light, we will never fully grasp the depth of our brokenness—or the overwhelming power of God's grace to heal it.

Scripture tells us, "The wages of sin is death" (Romans 6:23). The consequence of sin isn't a slap on the wrist or a divine timeout—it's death. Not just physical death, but spiritual and eternal death. That's not metaphorical. That's existential. That's real.

Only when we grasp the depravity of sin can we begin to understand the power of redemption—what it truly means to be saved. If we treat sin as trivial, we'll treat grace as cheap. But when the weight of sin hits us, we begin to see why we need a *Savior*, not just a cosmic referee.

And when that understanding moves from our heads to our hearts, something remarkable happens: The beautiful spirit of repentance begins to stir. Consider the Parable of the Prodigal Son. After exhausting himself in sin, he hits rock bottom—in a pigsty, covered in filth, longing to eat what the pigs are eating. And it's there, in the lowest place, that he remembers something profound: He is the son of a good father.

That long-buried truth—the memory of his father's love—is what gives him the strength to rise, turn around, and begin the journey home. That journey has a name: *repentance*. And it will be the focus of our next chapter.

Chapter 8

Repentance as Gift

There will be more joy in heaven over one sinner who repents than over ninety-nine righteous persons who need no repentance.
Luke 15:7

If my people who are called by my name humble themselves, pray, seek my face, and turn from their wicked ways, then I will hear from heaven, and will forgive their sin and heal their land.
2 Chronicles 7:14

Shortly after my wife and I got married, we moved to a small town in County Donegal, Ireland. The country is known for its almost endless rain, but one winter surprised us with a heavy snowfall. From our back window, the yard looked beautiful—covered in a thick, untouched blanket of white.

But as the days passed and the snow began to melt, something caught my eye. The handle of my son's tricycle was poking through, lying on its side. I crunched across the icy ground, pulled it out, and put it in the garage.

Over the next few weeks, as more snow melted, other things began to appear—forgotten toys, a few bottles and cans scattered around. The backyard I thought was pristine was actually cluttered and messy. It just took the snow melting to see it clearly. I realized then: It was time to clean it up.

I share that story because it reminds me of the way many of us first come to Jesus—we think we're doing alright. We figure we're decent people. Maybe we're aware of our temper, or we struggle with lust, and we want help. But overall, we assume we're in pretty good shape.

Then we start praying. We begin receiving the sacraments. We try to live a life of faith. And something happens. Slowly, as the light of God's grace begins to shine into the soul, the ice starts to thaw—and what's been buried begins to surface. We begin to see how much is broken, how much is disordered, how deep the sin really goes.

As C.S. Lewis put it:

> No man knows how bad he is till he has tried very hard to be good. . . . We never find out the strength of the evil impulse

inside us until we try to fight it: and Christ, because He was the only man who never yielded to temptation, is also the only man who knows to the full what temptation means—the only complete realist.[32]

That's the strange grace of the spiritual life: When we finally try to be holy, we discover how unholy we are. And like St. Paul, we find ourselves crying out: "Wretched man that I am! Who will deliver me from this body of death?" (Romans 7:24).

As we get to know Christ—and as we begin to take shelter in His refuge—this process truly begins. Our conscience sharpens. We start to notice things we hadn't before. The light doesn't just expose what's wrong; it helps us begin to see what holiness could actually look like.

I've always loved this line from Mark Twain: "Man is the only animal that blushes. Or needs to."[33]

It's a clever line, but it carries a deep insight about the human condition. Shame and guilt—those inward aches that make us want to hide—are part of our moral wiring. They signal that something within us knows right from wrong. Animals don't have this. They act on instinct. They feel no

---

[32] C.S.Lewis, *Mere Christianity* (The Macmillan Company, 1960), 109.
[33] Mark Twain, *Following the Equator* (Dover Publications, 1989), 256.

guilt, no shame, no remorse. But we do—because we're moral beings. And when we're confronted with our sin—when the mask slips and the truth is exposed—we feel it in our bones. We lower our eyes. We blush.

The reason we blush runs deeper than most people think. Some might assume it's just fear—that we're embarrassed because we know God sees all things and can punish sin. And while that's partly true, I think it misses the heart of it. We blush because, deep down, we know we were made for more. There's a dignity in us—a divine worth woven into our being. Shame, in that sense, is not just fear of punishment. It's sorrow for having fallen short of who we were made to be. It's the ache of a soul that remembers, even if dimly, its true home and its true self.

Seen in this light, we blush and feel shame not simply because we fear punishment, but because we know we were made for more. Shame isn't just guilt exposed; it's the sorrow of having fallen short of something higher, something noble. Deep down, we sense it: we were meant to be better than this. That sense of dignity isn't something we invented. God breathed it into us at the moment of our conception. As Christians, we believe that every human being, no matter where they live, what they believe, or how they act, bears the image and likeness of God (see Genesis 1:26–27).

The Blushing Prodigal

Shame and guilt are not ends in themselves. We're not meant to wallow in them. They're meant to wake us up—to shake us, gently or forcefully, into the truth. When received with humility, they become springboards to repentance and conversion. They stir in us a holy sorrow and turn our eyes back to the Father.

And here's what I want you to know: Repentance is beautiful.

That's not just my opinion—it's how Jesus sees it: "There will be more joy in heaven over one sinner who repents than over ninety-nine righteous persons who need no repentance" (Luke 15:7).

In the Parable of the Prodigal Son, we witness a sacred moment: In the filth of the pigsty, the son remembered who he was. He recalled his God-given dignity and began the long walk home to his father's love (see Luke 15:11–32). He knew he had sinned deeply. He knew he wasn't who he could be. But no matter how far he had fallen, there remained something in him that sin could not erase.

Repentance means more than feeling sorry for sin. It's a joyful awakening to the truth, a coming to our senses. A return to who we truly are: the beloved children of a merciful Father.

The decision to return to the father was beautiful because it was a return to his true identity—a son, still worthy of love, even after everything he'd done. It was beautiful because it was honest. In the pigsty, the prodigal didn't make excuses or shift blame. He faced his failure. And in that moment of vulnerability, he saw the deepest truth of his life: the Father's love was greater than his sin.

A powerful passage from the writings of St. Catherine of Siena comes to mind. Jesus told her that when our conscience reveals our sin, we must not despair—but trust in His mercy. Jesus said: "My mercy . . . is without any comparison greater than all the sins that are committed in the world."[34]

Is Repentance a Gift of God?

The New Testament Book of Acts makes a powerful claim about repentance—one that comes from a moment in St. Peter's life as he preached the Gospel to the Gentiles.

After Jesus ascended into Heaven, the early Church was faced with a question they hadn't yet answered, and it quickly became the theological elephant in the room. The first Christians were devout Jews, steeped in the traditions of their people. One of those traditions was clear: They did not regularly associate with Gentiles, in order to remain ritually "clean." But now Jesus had commanded them to preach the Gospel to all nations (see Luke 24:47). That meant stepping into Gentile homes, sharing meals, crossing boundaries. In short, someone was going to have to get "dirty."

The New Testament recounts that Peter received a

---

[34] Catherine of Siena, *The Dialogue of St. Catherine* (London, 1896), 296.

vision instructing him to go to Caesarea and minister to a group of Gentiles living there. He obeyed—and while he was speaking to them, the Holy Spirit came upon them (see Acts 11:15). Peter witnessed firsthand their repentance and their embrace of the Christian life. Deeply moved, he returned to Jerusalem and gathered the Church to share what he had seen. As he recounted how the Spirit had fallen on the Gentiles just as it had on them, the community was stunned. The room fell silent as the weight of it all sank in. Next Scripture tells us: "They praised God, saying, 'Then God has given even to the Gentiles the repentance that leads to life'" (Acts 11:18).

I like to think of the spirit of repentance as a gift— something the Holy Spirit gently stirs in the soul. The Spirit of God visits even the pigsties of our sin and breathes this grace into hearts willing to receive it. If only we would listen and respond!

The Acts of the Apostles gives us the theological truth: Repentance is a gift. But the Gospel of Luke makes that truth personal. As Jesus hung on the Cross, with His final breaths, He made a stunning promise to a man dying beside Him—a criminal we now know as St. Dismas.

Dismas the Thief

We meet Dismas only at the very end of his life. We don't know where he came from, what kind of family he had, or what led him down the path that ended in crucifixion. His crimes are never spelled out. But we do know his final words—and those last, sacred minutes of his life. Luke records them for us, likely having heard the account directly from the Apostle John and the Blessed Mother, who stood at the foot of the Cross and witnessed it all.

Luke tells the story like this:

> One of the criminals who were hanged there kept deriding him and saying, "Are you not the Messiah? Save yourself and us!" But the other rebuked him, saying, "Do you not fear God, since you are under the same sentence of condemnation? And we indeed have been condemned justly, for we are getting what we deserve for our deeds, but this man has done nothing wrong." Then he said, "Jesus, remember me when you come into your kingdom." He replied, "Truly I tell you, today you will be with me in Paradise." (Luke 23:39–43)

The words of Jesus—so rich with mercy, so radiant with glory—should bring tears to our eyes.

Tradition has long held, with a touch of humor, that Dismas "stole heaven." It seems his habit of thievery stayed with him to the very end. Throughout his life, he may have stolen many things of value, but nothing compares to the last thing he took: eternal life.

And yet, beneath the humor lies something profound. This moment reveals deep and beautiful truths about the heart of God.

First of all, God's love is so vast, so unconditional, that Dismas's entire life of sin was swept away in a single moment of grace. Fr. Jean d'Elbée offers a moving reflection on this moment. He writes: "A whole life of crimes, a whole life of sin: a few minutes before dying, one word of humility and confidence, and he is saved."[35]

Even as he hung dying, Jesus remained the Savior He had always been—merciful, attentive, full of love. On the Cross, He looked upon Dismas not with judgment, but with compassion, and He saved him. Fr. d'Elbée, in one of the most tender meditations on this scene, dares to imagine what passed through the heart of Christ at that moment. As if reading His thoughts, Fr. d'Elbée writes:

> For you, no Hell, not a second of Purgatory. The confident look you gave me, this meeting of our eyes, in my mercy and in your faith, has purified you in an instant and rendered us inseparable. Now you are completely pure and already in Heaven.[36]

---

[35] *I Believe in Love*, 36.

[36] *I Believe in Love*, 36.

It's a staggering vision of divine mercy—one that reminds us that even in our final hour, a single act of trust can open wide the gates of paradise.

The devil wants us to believe that a lifetime spent far from God requires a lifetime of penance to make things right. If we listen to that sinister voice—accusing, relentless—we begin to despair. It starts to seem as though there isn't enough time left to repent, not enough goodness in us to satisfy God's justice. But that voice is a lie.

There's something almost disorienting about the love of God. It's overwhelming—and, in a way, unsettling. It catches us off guard with its imbalance. As I mentioned earlier, part of us might prefer a harsher God—one who demands we earn our way back with long suffering and hard work. But that's not who He is.

Dismas, in his final moments, shut out the lies of the evil one and listened instead to Jesus' voice. But where did he find the strength and faith to do that? Perhaps we can look to the Blessed Mother, standing at the foot of the Cross. Could it be that, once again, she was interceding—asking her Son, as she had at Cana, to come to someone's aid? To turn the last moments of this man's broken life into something beautiful? To save the best for last?

Another profound truth we learn from the story of Dismas is that he was saved through humility and confidence. He had nothing to offer God but a broken heart. No good works to boast of, no noble words to impress. All he could do was throw himself into the arms of mercy. And he did. That act of surrender came through his repentance, his faith in Jesus, and his quiet, humble confidence in the love of Christ.

When we feel the weight of our sins—when we see our own misery—we should call to mind the final moments of Dismas's life. His example isn't just for deathbeds; it's for daily life. Each morning, we can begin again as he did, turning to Jesus in prayer with humility and confidence, speaking simply and briefly, but with trust. Like Dismas, we bring nothing but our need—and Christ meets us there with mercy.

Dismas did nothing to earn paradise—he simply trusted in Jesus. By walking the path of humility and trust, he became a saint. In the end, the most important truth about Dismas wasn't that he was a thief—it was that he was loved by God. Paraphrasing Thomas à Kempis,[37] we might say: "Whoever we are in the eyes of God, that we are—and nothing more."

Thérèse Takes the Elevator

Trusting God and embracing a humble, simple way of life are also the hallmarks of another great saint: St. Thérèse of Lisieux. I want to share with you a place of refuge she discovered—and how she faced her own imperfections and brokenness. Though

---

[37] See Thomas à Kempis, *The Imitation of Christ*, Book 2, Chapter 6: "You are what you are, and you cannot be said to be better than you are in God's sight."

she died at just twenty-four, her writings are filled with extraordinary spiritual insight. God accomplished great things through her—not in spite of her littleness, but because of it.

The heart of Thérèse's spirituality—and the reason for her lasting influence—is what she called her "little way." And interestingly, that little way began with an elevator. Today, elevators are so common we hardly notice them. But at the time, they were a new and remarkable invention.

Thérèse first encountered one while staying at a hotel in Rome during a pilgrimage to the Vatican with her family. The hotel's elegant lift made a strong impression on her young imagination. Later, back in France, she reflected on the experience and gave it a spiritual meaning. She wrote:

> We are living now in an age of inventions, and we no longer have to take the trouble of climbing stairs, for, in the homes of the rich, an elevator has replaced these very successfully. I wanted to find an elevator which would raise me to Jesus, for I am too small to climb the rough stairway of perfection.[38]

The image runs deeper than it might first appear. Thérèse was searching for a way to reach

---

[38] Thérèse of Lisieux, *Story of a Soul* (ICS Publications, 1976), 207.

Jesus—not by climbing the steep stairs of spiritual greatness, but by finding another path. In her heart, she sensed there had to be a "shortcut," some kind of elevator that could lift her to God. In her diary, she wrote:

> I searched, then, in the Scriptures for some sign of this elevator, the object of my desires, and I read these words coming from the mouth of Eternal Wisdom: 'Whoever is a LITTLE ONE, let him come to me." (Proverbs 9:4) And so I succeeded. I felt I had found what I was looking for. But wanting to know, O my God, what You would do to *the very little one* who answered Your call, I continued my search and this is what I discovered: 'As one whom a mother caresses, so will I comfort you; you shall be carried at the breasts, and upon the knees they shall caress you.' (Isaiah 66:13,12) Ah! never did words more tender and more melodious come to give joy to my soul. The elevator which must raise me to heaven is Your arms, O Jesus! And for this I had no need to grow up, but rather I had to remain *little* and become this more and more.[39]

For Thérèse, the elevator was the arms of Jesus.

---

[39] *Story of a Soul,* 207.

She would remain little, and He would lift her up. It wasn't about striving or proving herself—it was about trusting completely in His mercy. With bold confidence in God's love, she chose a life of humility and simplicity, anchored in trust.

But Thérèse's image of the elevator doesn't exist in isolation. Every elevator, after all, has a staircase beside it. And in her metaphor, the stairs represent the temptation to rely on ourselves—to climb by our own strength, our own virtue, our own willpower. To choose the stairs over the elevator is to seek a false refuge. It's the subtle pride of thinking we can reach God on our own.

What does this mean for the spiritual life? What's actually happening when we try to take the stairs?

At its core, trying to climb the stairs is treating Christianity as if it were merely a system of rules—a demanding moral code marked by strict norms and a drive toward perfectionism. You can certainly try to go it alone, striving hard to root out vice and cultivate virtue. And you might make some progress. But in the end, you can only climb so high on your own strength. The stairs don't reach heaven.

Another thing that happens when we take the stairs is that we try to take control. Elevators, after all, don't give us much control. Aside from pressing a button, we're at their mercy. Have you ever had that odd experience in a tall building—trying to go down, only for the elevator to take you up? Or stopping on a dozen random floors before you reach your own?

It's tempting to take the stairs instead. They feel more predictable, more manageable. They seem safer.

Isn't that what we do in the spiritual life? When we try to seize control—forcing outcomes, clinging to our own plans—we're choosing the stairs. We want to climb on our terms, at our pace, instead of surrendering to the God who lifts us in His time, by His grace.

When we trust in God's mercy and stop trying to manage everything on our own, we begin to let Him take full control of our lives. And like an elevator, His path may include unexpected ups and downs. Giving God that kind of permission isn't easy—it requires surrender. But it's the only way. No one climbs their way to heaven.

The prodigal son, like Thérèse, let go of his old ways. He came home empty-handed, and the father welcomed him—not with scolding, but with joy. His return began the moment he "stepped into the elevator" of God's love and became little. That's where the journey home always begins.

Dismas the Thief came home, too. He had spent a lifetime far from the Father—but the Father was only a breath away, waiting for that very moment. Dismas became "little" when he surrendered in trust and love to Jesus. And in that instant, Jesus gave him paradise.

The beauty of this homecoming—this return to the Father's embrace—is what we'll explore in the next chapter.

Chapter 9

Refuge Found

*The Lord is a refuge for the oppressed,
a stronghold in times of trouble.*
Psalm 9:9

F inding refuge in Christ—coming home to
Him and receiving the warmth of the Father's
love and grace—is a profound experience. It may
sound bold to say, but in my experience, there is
no life more beautiful than one lived in the refuge
Christ offers. Nothing else compares. Returning
to Christ, or arriving for the very first time, pro-
vides deep and lasting realities that mark our
souls. Words cannot express the emotion and

transformation that occurs in someone who has returned to Christ.

It's worth noting that while emotions often accompany this return, they aren't the measure of its truth. Feelings may come and go, but the grace of refuge runs deeper than our emotional landscape. We don't judge our nearness to Christ by what we feel, but by the faith with which we return to Him.

In this chapter, I want to reflect on the experience of coming home to that refuge—not just emotionally, but spiritually and practically. I will focus on the return experience of the Prodigal Son. This parable has woven its way through much of this book, and rightly so—it is one of the most powerful portrayals of the spiritual journey of conversion and homecoming. As a piece of inspired Scripture, it never runs dry. For those willing to listen, it continues to offer an abundance of insight—into the heart of God, into ourselves, and into life in this world.

In the last chapter, we arrived at the wayward son's homecoming. The grace of his repentance carried him from the pigsty back toward his homeland. But what awaited him there was nothing like he had imagined—and that, for us, is wonderfully good news. Our own returns to God may be just as surprising.

In Jesus' parable, the son encounters two things he wasn't expecting.

The First Surprise

First, the son was surprised by *where* he met his father. Luke tells us the encounter happened "while he was still a long way off" (Luke 15:20). Why? Because the father had been watching the horizon—waiting, hoping, scanning the distance for the silhouette of his child. The son had assumed he'd have to make the full journey home, step-by-painful step. But he didn't. His father ran to meet him. The love of the father bridged the gap.

In this part of the parable, Jesus reveals something profound about the love of God the Father: He doesn't wait passively for our return. Like the father in the story, He rushes toward us. He crosses any distance to reach His lost children.

The Church has long cherished a passage from the Book of Wisdom, read each year at Midnight Mass. In it, we glimpse the moment of the Incarnation—the moment Jesus "leaps" from heaven to earth to find us:

> For while gentle silence enveloped all things, and night in its swift course was now half gone,
> your all-powerful word leaped from heaven, from the royal throne, into the midst of the land that was doomed.
> (Wisdom 18:14–15)

On our own journey back to the Father, we can be sure of this: We're not walking alone. At every turn, the

Father is already watching for us, already drawing near.

The Second Surprise

The prodigal son's second surprise was *how* he met his father. He expected anger, perhaps even rejection. At best, he hoped to be allowed back as a servant—a kind of second-class son. On the road home, he rehearsed the speech he planned to give. After all, he had a lot to atone for. He had burned bridges, and he knew it. Luke tells us he even prepared the exact words he would say:

> Father, I have sinned against heaven and before you. I am no longer worthy to be called your son. (Luke 15:21)

And yet, surprisingly, the father paid no attention to his son's carefully rehearsed apology. He didn't respond to the excuses or the pleas. There was no rebuke, no lecture, no trial or conditions for reentry. The father wasn't angry—he was overwhelmed with relief. All he had ever wanted was for his son to come home. You can almost see the tears in his eyes as he turned quickly to the servants and commanded them to clothe his son in fine garments and prepare a feast.

And then came the father's words: "Let us eat and celebrate. For this my son was dead, and is alive again; he was lost, and is found" (Luke 15:23–24).

Like the prodigal son, when we return home to the

Father, when we enter into the refuge that is Jesus, so many wonderful graces await us. Fr. d'Elbee says,

> Remember that, each time you pick yourself up after a fall, the feast of the prodigal son is renewed. Your Father in heaven clothes you again in His most beautiful cloak, puts a ring on your finger, and tells you to dance with joy. In a living faith, you will not approach the confessional with dragging feet, but as if you were going to a feast.[40]

Jesus is always inviting us to the feast. He has set the table with abundant spiritual gifts and graces, and He extends that invitation to us each and every day. It is an invitation to the deepest love possible.

The Unbounded Love of God

Above all, the central experience of embracing the refuge Christ offers is to be enveloped by the unbounded love of God. This is, without question, the most astounding part of "coming home." God is not stingy with His love, as we are apt to be. His love is given so freely and overwhelmingly that we will spend all of eternity rejoicing in this love. God has promised us this, even since the days of the Old Testament:

---

[40] *I Believe in Love*, 34.

And the ransomed of the Lord shall return
    and come to Zion with singing;
  everlasting joy shall be upon their heads;
    they shall obtain gladness and joy,
    and sorrow and sighing shall flee away.
(Isaiah 35:10)

In the Gospel parable, the prodigal son was stunned into silence by this overwhelming love. He had spoken many words in his life—some harsh, some foolish—especially toward his father and brother. But now, faced with the father's mercy, he said nothing. The parable records no further words from him. He wasn't allowed to grovel or plead. He was simply taken by the hand and led into the father's house. The only thing left for him to do was rejoice.

I imagine the prodigal son had a hard time wrapping his heart and mind around what was happening. None of it followed human logic. He had likely prepared himself for a harsh confrontation—perhaps a cold stare, a list of conditions, or a long path to earn back favor. If we're honest, that's how many of us would respond if *we* were the father in the story. We'd want apologies, explanations. We'd want the son to feel the weight of what he'd done.

But mercifully, God is not like us.

God is perfectly just—but we often confuse justice with harshness. We tend to be rigid, quick to judge, slow to forgive. We keep records. We expect people to earn their way back. Deep down, we think we deserve God's anger, not His love—and we're right. We *do* deserve it. We've sinned. We've turned away from Him.

But astonishingly, God's response is not punishment—it's love. Not rejection, but embrace. His answer to our guilt is mercy. His answer to our failure is Himself. And this, dear reader, is why we call Christianity good news! And how good it is! I've often felt that the real challenge of Christianity isn't that it's too hard to believe—but that it's *too good* to believe. How can anything be this good? We've all been burned before—we've trusted promises that fell apart, believed in people who let us down. So when we hear of a love that is total, a mercy that knows no limits, something in us resists. *Could this really be true? Could something so beautiful actually hold up?*

This is where the story of Naaman the Syrian can speak to us. His story begins not with faith, but with disbelief. And yet, even in that, God was at work. The account opens with these words:

> Naaman, commander of the army of the king of Syria, was a great man with his master and in high favor, because by him the Lord had given victory to Syria. He was a mighty man of valor, but he was a leper (2 Kings 5:1).

In the story of Naaman, we see a striking contrast: greatness and leprosy, side by side. Leprosy might seem ordinary in a poor, forgotten man—but not in the commander of an army. And yet, there it was, eating away at Naaman's strength, threatening to undo his power, his pride, and eventually, his life. Desperate and humbled, the great general heard of a prophet in Israel—Elisha—and set out in hope of a miracle.

Naaman didn't know the God of Israel. He assumed that healing must come at a high price, so he arrived with an extravagant offering: "ten talents of silver, six thousand shekels of gold, and ten changes of clothing" (2 Kings 5:5). But Naaman was mistaken. God is not like us. He doesn't barter or bargain. His gifts are given freely, not earned. What God desires is not wealth or status, but relationship. Naaman didn't need to bring treasure—he needed to bring an honest, humble heart.

Naaman's misunderstanding of God became a stumbling block. When he finally met the prophet Elisha, he was caught off guard—not by some dramatic miracle, but by what seemed an almost insulting simplicity. Elisha didn't even come out to greet him. Instead, he sent a message:

Naaman came with his horses and chariots and stood at the door of Elisha's house. And Elisha sent a messenger to him, saying, "Go and wash in the Jordan seven times, and your flesh shall be restored, and you shall be clean." (2 Kings 5:9–10)

Naaman was insulted by the simplicity of the command. After journeying a great distance—passing by countless rivers and arriving with expectation—he was told to wash in the Jordan, a modest and unimpressive river compared to those of his homeland. It seemed beneath him. Offended and angry, he was ready to abandon the very healing he came to find. But his attendants saw what pride was blinding him to. They gently urged him to reconsider, pointing out the irony: If the prophet had asked him to do something difficult—scale a mountain or prove his strength—he would have done it without hesitation. So why refuse when the task was so small?

Naaman was persuaded, and so "he went down and dipped himself seven times in the Jordan, according to the word of the man of God, and his flesh was restored like the flesh of a little child, and he was clean" (2 Kings 5:14).

Naaman's healing and cure came at almost no cost to himself. He was overwhelmed and was now a believer. He testified: "Behold, I know that there is no God in all the earth but in Israel" (2 Kings 5:15).

Like Naaman, we may struggle to believe that God truly loves us—that the salvation and refuge He offers, free and undeserved, is somehow too good to be true. The devil, the accuser, whispers that we're not lovable, that at best, God merely tolerates us. He wants us to believe that God is like us: cold, exacting, slow to forgive.

But God shatters that lie. His mercy is not earned. It is given. And our part is simple, like Naaman's: to trust, and to be confident in His love.

I love this passage from Fr. Robert H. Benson's

book *The Friendship of Christ*. He does not say where he found it, just that it was "from an old manuscript." Whoever wrote it has truly experienced this overwhelming love of God, having returned to the embrace of the Father and experienced the relieved "tears" of God.

THIS IS MY FRIEND

Let me tell you how I made His acquaintance.
I had heard much of Him, but took no heed.
He sent daily gifts and presents, but I never thanked Him.
He often seemed to want my friendship, but I remained cold.
I was homeless, and wretched, and starving and in peril every hour; and He offered me shelter and comfort and food and safety; but I was ungrateful still.
At last He crossed my path and with tears in His eyes He besought me saying, Come and abide with me.

Let me tell you how he treats me now.
He supplies all my wants.
He gives me more than I dare ask.
He anticipates my every need.
He begs me to ask for more.
He never reminds me of my past ingratitude.
He never rebukes me for my past follies.

Let me tell you further what I think of Him.
 He is as good as He is great.
 His love is as ardent as it is true.
 He is as lavish of His promises as He is faithful in keeping them.
 He is as jealous of my love as He is deserving of it.
 I am in all things His debtor, but He bids me call Him Friend.

A Necessary Caveat

We turn now to a necessary caveat that must be shared on the experience of coming home to God. It is this: Just because we have returned to God does not mean our lives on earth will now be easy and without hardship.

We must admit that the lives of devout Christians and the historical witness of the saints can be, and often were, full of crosses. If your life now is full of hardship, please know that this does not mean you are far from God. Rather, a Christian may find that sufferings in life can, by God's grace, unite us more closely to the Crucified Lord.

To shed some light on this topic, I want to invite another saint into this book, one who has left a powerful impact on the Church: Venerable Cardinal Francis-Xavier Nguyen Van Thuan.

Cardinal Van Thuan was at first just a young bishop in Vietnam, quietly taking care of his flock.

He did so for eight years. And then his life was forever changed. He was swept up in the wars and chaos of his time when he was named coadjutor archbishop of Saigon in 1975.

Cardinal Van Thuan arrived in the city just as the communist forces were approaching Saigon. Seven days after he arrived to begin his work, the city fell to the communists. While the world watched in shock as the images of the humanitarian crisis unfolded, there in the middle of it all was the forty-seven-year-old bishop, trying to help his flock.

A short three months later, before Cardinal Van Thaun was even able to get started, he was arrested by the communists and sent to prison. He was stripped of his flock, he could not govern his diocese, and he could not speak freely to his people. He felt he had abandoned the people God had placed under his care.

Thus, in prison, Cardinal Van Thuan experienced the deepest personal hardships of his life. There, in the darkness, God met him. In his memorable book, *Five Loaves and Two Fish*, he writes about an inner experience of God's presence during his time in prison:

> One night, from the depths of my heart I could hear a voice advising me: "Why torment yourself? You must discern between God and the works of God. Everything you have done and desire to

continue to do, pastoral visits, training seminarians, sisters and members of religious orders, building schools, evangelizing non-Christians. All of that is excellent work, the work of God but it is not God! If God wants you to give it all up and put the work into his hands, do it and trust him. God will do the work infinitely better than you; he will entrust the work to others who are more able than you. You have only to choose God and not the works of God!"[41]

Cardinal Van Thuan realized that Jesus Himself, while He died on the Cross in a divine act of love, was, like the cardinal himself, unable to speak, unable to heal, unable to preach with words. Because of this revelation, Cardinal Van Thuan received a peace of soul, despite the awful circumstances of imprisonment.

He was finally released from prison in 1988 and would spend the remaining fourteen years of his life sharing his story with the world.

Why do I bring up Cardinal Van Thuan?

It is because, despite the awfulness of his imprisonment and the harsh conditions, his heart was still able to sing of God's love. He could not be shaken, ever. The world around him was falling

---

[41] Francis-Xavier Nguyen Van Thuan, *Five Loaves and Two Fish* (Catholic Truth Society, 2009), 17.

apart, and Cardinal Van Thuan was still anchored in the refuge of Christ. Cardinal Van Thuan had no easy road to walk, but as he was walking with Christ, nothing else mattered. He had entered into that state of love and peace that only comes from refuge in Christ.

I'm reminded of a particularly powerful passage from the *Imitation of Christ*:

> Love is a great thing, a great good in every way, for it alone lightens every burden and passes smoothly over all misfortunes. Love carries a burden without feeling it and makes every bitter thing sweet and savory.... A person who loves may soar, run and rejoice; he is free and nothing holds him back. . . . Love often knows no limit, but exceeds all limits. Love feels no burden, shrugs off all labor, aims beyond its strength, and refuses to admit impossibility. Because love believes that it can accomplish anything, it does.[42]

Already, but Not Yet

I want to end this chapter with an important distinction. As I've stated, finding refuge in Christ does not mean all our problems will vanish in this life. Like the imprisoned Cardinal Van Thuan, we're not in

---

[42] Thomas a Kempis, *Imitation of Christ*, III, 5.

Heaven yet—and Jesus never promised a pain-free life here on earth.

To understand this, here is a key truth of the Christian life: The fullness of life in Christ is something we taste partially now but will experience fully in Heaven. Theologians often describe this reality with a simple phrase: *Already, but not yet.*

Through Baptism, divine life has *already* been given to us. We truly are children of God. But that life hasn't fully blossomed—*not yet*. We walk with Christ now, yes, but we still await the day when Jesus "will wipe away every tear from their eyes, and death shall be no more, neither shall there be mourning, nor crying, nor pain anymore, for the former things have passed away" (Revelation 21:4).

On earth, we don't see God face-to-face. St. Paul speaks about this in one of his letters: "For now we see in a mirror dimly, but then face to face. Now I know in part; then I shall know fully, even as I have been fully known" (1 Corinthians 13:12).

By saying "already," we mean that God has already poured his abundant graces and participation in divine life upon us. By saying "not yet," we mean that on this side of heaven, the graces are not yet fully in act.

This tension between the *already* and the *not yet* is at the heart of the Catholic experience. We are already saved by Christ, yet we await our definitive entrance into Heaven with the saints of God.

We are already loved beyond measure, yet we struggle to live worthy of that love.

We are already healed by Christ, yet we still suffer the pain of earthly wounds and sin.

In short, while the refuge of Christ is the only true answer to the deepest yearnings of the human heart, it does not magically erase life's difficulties. But it does make those difficulties worth enduring.

But There's More

So what now? What do we do while *already* living in grace, but *not yet* in the fullness of glory? Is there more to say—more to do—while we wait in the refuge of Christ, longing for our heavenly home?

The answer to that will be found in the next chapter.

Chapter 10

Sharing Our Divine Refuge

Blessed are the merciful, for they shall obtain mercy.
Matthew 5:7

Learn from me, for I am gentle and lowly in heart.
Matthew 11:29

T hose of us who have been raised in the West have
grown up in a culture that in many ways is indifferent or hostile to the Christian faith.

It is indifferent because of its relativism. People
widely assume that all truth is a matter of personal
opinion.

It is hostile because of its antagonism toward God.
Deep down, the cities of men oppose the city of God.

Many Christians have opted to go along with this

culture and are living out their faith privately, keeping their beliefs safely tucked away from public view. While they may attend a church on Sunday, the rest of the week they live just as their nonreligious neighbors do.

On a personal level, this type of life becomes an obstacle to grace. On a community level, a church that is afraid and locks itself behind closed doors will remain unsure of its mission and lose its ability to bring people to Christ.

But hiding one's faith is a problem. The refuge that Christ offers cannot be conceived of as a private affair between Jesus and the individual soul. The salvation offered by Christ is meant to be offered to all persons. The refuge we enter into is also a refuge that is meant to be shared. Thus, when Christians privatize their religion, they are closing off the offering of salvation to others. Think of it this way: None of us are a Christian because of our own efforts. In all our lives, we became Christians because somebody talked to us about Christ, a parent raised us in the faith, or at the very least we read or heard something, like a book or a podcast, that was written by another Christian. We all have a part to play in this work of evangelization. We all are to invite others into the refuge of Christ.

An Invitation to More

Today, as always, Christ wishes to meet us

anew. He wants to cross our path, to meet us where we are. Christ stands before us with open arms. The power of His grace is as strong as ever, and in fact, the farther we are from God, the more grace is at work: "Where sin increased, grace abounded all the more" (Romans 5:20).

At the end of this book, I pray that no matter how far you are from God, you will hear Jesus' invitation to come home, to enter our good Father's house.

Jesus gives eternal salvation freely and invites every person, no matter their past, to come to Him for refuge today. On the very last page of Scripture, in the end of the Book of Revelation, Jesus gives us one last invitation: "Let everyone who is thirsty come. Let anyone who wishes take the water of life as a gift" (Revelation 22:17, NRSV).

We are all thirsting for this water. To be human is to want this drink. And it's free! Every day, the Church, in her sacraments and her treasury of grace, makes this drink available to us. It's ours for the taking!

The water of life is a free gift that cannot be purchased. Truly, there is nothing we can do to repay Our Lord for the refuge He has provided for us. While we can't "repay" Jesus, there are certain attitudes and actions we can do to at least express our desire to thank Him. All four Gospels record a story of a woman who wanted to thank or "repay" Our Lord, a woman with a flask of perfume.

Breaking Our Flasks

This woman lived in or near Bethany. While St. John calls her Mary (see John 12:3), the other Gospels leave her nameless. Luke goes so far as to say she was a sinful woman (see Luke 7:37).

She met Jesus in Bethany, their meeting occurring in the days leading up to Good Friday. On this day:

> A woman came with an alabaster flask
> of ointment of pure nard, very costly,
> and she broke the flask and poured it
> over his head.
> (Mark 14:3)

I love this image of "breaking the flask." This woman gave her very expensive perfumed oil completely to Jesus. She broke the flask, holding nothing back, and there was no turning back. All was for Jesus.

We can only speculate as to what her sin could have been or what disease Jesus might have healed her from. For her forgiveness, healing, or both, she was grateful. And she felt inclined to do something for Jesus. While she couldn't actually *repay* Jesus, she did what her human heart told her to do: She made a radical offering of the best that she had. Anointing Jesus symbolized the love she had for Our Lord. Her life was now all for Jesus. No fear, no reservation, no concern for the opinions of others would get in the way.

She did not worry about tomorrow or what she would do without her treasured perfume. Our Lord accepted her gift—her love—without hesitation, and in that sacred exchange, this woman found divine refuge.

This woman's anointing of Jesus was more than a nice gesture—it held within it a secret of the Catholic saints. Like Mary, the saints are those who perceive a need to "console Our Lord." They want to give back to Jesus, not just take. In this way, the saints don't just "use" religion for their own benefit. Instead, they plumb the depths of the Christian faith by entering into the mystery of life *in* Christ, life *with* Christ, life *because* of Christ, and life *for* Christ. St. Paul, in pursuing this life of sacrificial giving, even said: "I rejoice in my sufferings for your sake, and in my flesh I am filling up what is lacking in Christ's afflictions" (Colossians 1:24).

Consoling the Heart of Jesus

This woman's attitude, her choice to hold nothing back from Jesus, is one that we should adopt as we can. In some way, she seems to have intuited that Jesus' heart was heavy because of His impending Passion and death. And therefore, she wanted to suffer with Him, to be there for Him. She showed compassion, which in its Latin root means literally "suffering with." Jesus welcomed her love and her compassion.

Down through the centuries, what many of the Catholic saints have done for Christ is known as

"consoling the Heart of Jesus." This practice has
become a part of Church teaching. Pope Pius XI
took the notion of consoling Christ and put it into
doctrinal form. In 1928, he wrote:

> Now if, because of our sins also which
> were as yet in the future, but were fore-
> seen, the soul of Christ became sorrowful
> unto death, it cannot be doubted that
> then, too, already He derived somewhat
> of solace from our reparation, which was
> likewise foreseen, when "there appeared
> to Him an angel from heaven" (Luke
> 22:43), in order that His Heart, oppressed
> with weariness and anguish, might find
> consolation. And so even now, in a
> wondrous yet true manner, we can and
> ought to console that Most Sacred Heart
> which is continually wounded by the sins
> of thankless men.[43]

Much mystery still remains here. But we step
forward in our spiritual journey when we can take
on the role of the "angel from heaven" (Luke
22:43). In this moment, we stop just asking Jesus
for "stuff." We stop just complaining to God about
our difficulties. We arise from the various forms of
spiritual selfishness. And then we take a step
forward in spiritual growth. Here, we take notice of

[43] Pope Pius XI, *Miserentissimus Redemptor*, May 1928, 13.

God. We begin to hear the small requests of Jesus. We listen, and we heed His voice in our lives. Whatever alabaster jars of perfume we possess, we courageously break them and pour them out for God.

"Consoling the Heart of Jesus" also entails doing good to our fellow man. When we serve the people around us, we are also serving Jesus. As He said, "Truly, I say to you, as you did it to one of the least of these my brothers, you did it to me" (Matthew 25:40).

The Great Commission

In His final moments on earth, before His Ascension, Jesus gave us another command. He said:

> All authority in heaven and on earth has been given to me. Go therefore and make disciples of all nations, baptizing them in the name of the Father and of the Son and of the Holy Spirit, and teaching them to obey everything that I have commanded you. And remember, I am with you always, to the end of the age. (Matthew 28:18–20)

We can glean two key ideas from Jesus' words.

First, the mission to evangelize is paramount and central to the Gospel. Jesus gathered those men and women for a purpose: to go to the ends of the earth.

Second, Jesus does not want just a few people

saved. He wants all peoples to enter into the cosmic worship of God. There is no "us against them." In the end, we should be deeply saddened if a soul is lost to Hell. That's not what God wants, and no Christian should ever feel in their heart or say to themselves that someone or some group should just "go to Hell."

When we speak of evangelization, we mean a lot of things. Essentially, evangelization means sharing the Faith with others. As our most precious gift, eternal salvation is something we naturally should want to speak about and share. We are not sharing ideas, but rather a relationship we have with Christ. In this way, we invite others to seek refuge in Christ. The safe harbor we have found is the *only* safe harbor. As such, we must be a lighthouse in the storms of the world. We should help, direct, encourage, support and welcome all those in our life to refuge in Christ. All the while, fulfilling this great commission is our way of "consoling the Heart of Jesus."

At the conclusion of this book, I now want to gather the ideas and reflections I have made and offer them once again in a practical way. Here are five principles that will help us to share our refuge in Christ with the world.

The Five Principles
1. Renounce False Places of Refuge
In Chapter 6 we addressed many false places of refuge and made the commitment to renounce

them for the sake of Christ. A phrase from St. Therese will help us here: "The World is but a ship and not thy home."[44]

This was a phrase that the saint learned from her father, and she said this to herself in difficult moments. It has a timeless truth to it. When we try to make a paradise for ourselves here on earth, we are seeking out a false refuge.

This does not mean that we never enjoy the good things of life here on earth. By no means! The saints are often the happiest of people, people who know how to enjoy God's good creation. Even St. Thomas Aquinas, in the midst of his deep theological speculation, had his feet firmly on the ground. He was once asked "whether pain and sorrow are assuaged by sleep and baths?"[45] The saint answered in the affirmative! God has gifted us with our humanity, this beautiful union of a spiritual soul and a corporeal body. All that is good for the body (i.e., rest, nourishment, leisure, exercise) is good for the soul.

Yet everything taken to an extreme can become a problem. Distracting oneself by scrolling on a phone is not leisure. Gluttony is not nourishment, fornication is not love, and drunkenness is not happiness.

Even inside the refuge of Christ, while we are

---

[44] St. Thérèse of Lisieux, *The Story of a Soul* (Source Books, 1973), 73.

[45] Thomas Aquinas, *Summa Theologica*, I, II, 38.

here on this earth, we will need to be careful of seeking out false refuges. We are not magically immune to them just because we have opted for Christ. Instead, we are to carry our crosses, to shoulder our burdens, and to walk behind the Master, even when He walks the path of Calvary.

When these false places of refuge rear their ugly heads, we must renounce them. We must let them go. In the appendix of this book, I have placed a renunciation prayer that has helped me often.

2. Foster a Personal Relationship with Jesus Christ

The question that Jesus placed before us from Chapter 3 was: "Who do you say that I am?" (Matthew 16:13). This question needs to be answered by every individual person. Many Christians do not truly live their faith. They are registered at a parish, they may be sacramentalized (through Baptism, Confirmation, and Communion), they may know a few ideas about the Christian faith, but they don't have a real relationship with God. This is a quiet tragedy!

Jesus wants to offer us an abundance of life (John 10:10). He does not want to be an idea, but rather He wants to be *someone* for us. Our faith is a person. Without a real relationship with God that changes my everyday life, my faith won't be "shareable." Without a real relationship with God, expressed in regular prayer and sacramental life, there isn't growth or transformation. We drift away from God, seeking refuge in the world's cheap neon lights, forsaking a journey toward the good light of God's eternal dawn.

Honestly, one of the best things you can do for yourself, your family, and the world is to want to become a saint. This begins with a commitment to some form of daily prayer, sacramental life, and intentionality.

3. Trust Christ Forever

Once we are secure in the refuge of Christ and have a living faith, we will need to confront what can be a lifelong temptation. As we mentioned in Chapter 8, St. Thérèse provided us with two ways to approach the spiritual life: either taking the elevator or the stairs.

Taking the elevator is to trust in our good God, allowing His mercy to transform us.

Taking the stairs is to trust in ourselves. Sometimes we choose this because we are spiritually proud and have a pharisaical attitude about religion. Sometimes it is because we are despairing in our weaknesses and sins. We assume God couldn't love us because of our past and that we have to take the stairs to "earn" forgiveness in some way.

St. Thérèse will always be a model for those who fight to keep on trusting in God alone. The secret to the lives of the saints will always entail a complete trust in Jesus.

The devil hates that we grow closer to God. The devil hates the elevator, which can whisk away a soul from demonic despair and lies. The devil wants us to be afraid. He wants us to run from God, to hide under the shade of our existential fig trees. His lies tell us that we never deserved God's love to begin with.

Believing in love is hard. But it is essential. It is a gift to ask for, a grace to seek out. Take the elevator.

4. Work with the Paraclete, Not the Accuser

The devil is known as the "accuser." The Book of Revelation says:

> I heard a loud voice in heaven, saying, "Now the salvation and the power and the kingdom of our God and the authority of his Christ have come, for the accuser of our brothers has been thrown down, who accuses them day and night before our God." (Revelation 12:10)

The devil, as the accuser, tells lies, points fingers, obscures the truth, destroys, defames, and with poisonous words attempts to separate us from God.

The devil's behavior is the opposite of God's: "God did not send his Son into the world to condemn the world, but in order that the world might be saved through him" (John 3:17).

Jesus, as Savior, healed, loved, sacrificed, enlightened, encouraged, and with merciful words brought humanity back into union with God the Father. Jesus certainly warned us about sin. But He did so to give life.

Before He ascended into Heaven, Jesus promised to send us not an accuser, but an advocate, a "paraclete." He said: "I will ask the Father, and he will give you another Advocate, to be with you forever" (John 14:16).

As our Advocate, the Holy Spirit stands with us, not against us. He is not a prosecutor, but a defense attorney. The Holy Spirit is at our side with His shield to defend us in battle. We are never fighting God; we are fighting the devil, the evilness of the world, and our sinful nature. Like our Advocate, we too should strive to embody this way of being, especially in regard to evangelization. Our role in the world should also be to encourage and defend others, inviting and supporting all those who are on their journey home to refuge in Christ. The message that we share as Christians is the most beautiful message, the most healing balm, the greatest of stories and the most priceless gift!

Despite this, unfortunately, one of the stereotypical images of a Christian is someone who is judgmental, mean, accusatory, and threatening the world with apocalyptic doom. Sadly, we've all met Christians who lack empathy and compassion. The stereotypical "holier than thou" Christian has many real personifications. Perhaps these people are more akin to the older brother in the Parable of the Prodigal Son. This older brother can't allow the younger prodigal son to go unpunished. This is because, for the older son, his external obedience to the father *earns* him many rights and privileges. In his mind, the younger son has disobeyed and lost these privileges. As such, he must be punished forever.

The older son only sees justice and cannot see mercy. While the older son may never have abandoned the father's house, sadly, he has never really been home. This is immortalized in the parable by the elder son who stands on the porch of the father's house but does not go in. Even when the father pleads for him to celebrate and join the feast, his stubbornness keeps him spiritually far from home.

There are perhaps too many Christians who stand on the porch of God's home. Their rigidity, over-seriousness, and pride make them awful human beings. They fall into the sin of scandal, in that they give a false witness to the world about Christianity.

We would do much better to present the Good, the True, and the Beautiful to the world. This is the way of the Gospel—this is the faith. Jesus does not ask us to be His deputy sheriffs. In fact, He told His disciples, "Judge not, that you be not judged" (Matthew 7:1). He is asking us to be His hands and feet and voice, His love in the heart of the world.

Being love in the heart of the world is ultimately a call to love like Jesus. This love is boundless. It is commonly referred to as *magnanimity*, which literally means "greatness of soul."

5. Practice Humility

Many people understand humility as just the opposite of pride. But there is more to this virtue than meets the eye.

For one, humility is Christlike. Our Lord Himself gave us the greatest example of humility: His brutal death on a Roman cross.

Humility is also to walk in the truth. We shouldn't confuse humility with self-deprecation. Meekness is not weakness. The humble person has a proper understanding of who they are because they live their lives before the loving eyes of God.

Practicing humility is also a request from Jesus. He asked that we be humble and gentle of heart. He told us this in Matthew's Gospel. I believe Matthew, because of his strong personal conversion and subsequent friendship with Christ, was very moved when he heard these words that he later recorded in his Gospel:

> Take my yoke upon you, and learn from me, for I am gentle and lowly in heart, and you will find rest for your souls. For my yoke is easy, and my burden is light. (Matthew 11:29–30)

The yoke of Jesus is truly light. A life of sin and selfishness destroys, causing pain and despair. Life apart from Christ is unbearable. And many of our brothers and sisters in this world are suffering.

They need to know about the love and mercy of God.

I invite you to take up this yoke and to embrace a gentle and humble heart. This should be the hallmark of every Christian. If we only did this, the world would be a different place!

The Old Testament prophet Micah can give us a closing message. Of all the things we could do, of all the many tasks and projects that we are presented with, in the end, life on earth as a Christian is simple. As you go your way, I pray you will always live in the safe refuge that is Christ, heeding these words from Micah:

What does the Lord require of you?
Only this: to do what is right, to show mercy, and to walk humbly with your God.
(Micah 6:8, emphasis added)

Appendix I

A Treasury of
Spiritual Reflections

Every author stands on the shoulders of those who have come before. As I wrote this book, a number of great passages from the saints and spiritual authors spoke to me deeply. I want to include some of them here, perhaps for your time of prayer or morning reflections. I hope you enjoy them and are aided by them as much as I have been.

Fr. Jacques Philippe

"Mature" Christians, who have truly become children of God, are those who have experienced their radical nothingness, their absolute poverty, been reduced to nothing. At the bottom of that nothingness, they have finally discovered the inexpressible tenderness, the absolutely unconditional love, of God. Henceforth their only support and hope is the boundless mercy of their Father God.[46]

---

[46] *Interior Freedom* (Scepter Publishers, Inc., 2007), 129.

Jesus to St. Maria Faustina Kowalska

I perform works of mercy in every soul. The greater the sinner, the greater the right he has to My mercy. My mercy is confirmed in every work of My hands. He who trusts in My mercy will not perish, for all his affairs are Mine, and his enemies will be shattered at the base of My footstool.[47]

St. Elizabeth of the Trinity

Little sister of my soul, God is making me understand many things in the fight of eternity, and I want to tell you, as coming from Him, not to be afraid of sacrifice, of struggle, but on the contrary, to rejoice, if your nature is an occasion of strife, a battlefield. Do not be discouraged, nor distressed, in fact, I would say love your wretchedness, since it gives God an opportunity to exercise His mercy. In so far as the sight of your misery makes you depressed and turns you back upon yourself, it is the effect of self-love! In times of tribulation, take refuge in your Master's prayer. Yes, little sister, He saw you from His Cross, He prayed for you and "He lives on still to make intercession on our behalf." That prayer will save you from your wretchedness. The more you feel your weakness, the greater must grow your trust.[48]

---

[47] *Diary*, 723.
[48] *Spiritual Writings* (Kenedy & Sons, 1906), 116.

Blessed Columba Marmion

What, then, is mercy? Mercy is goodness or love which, in the presence of wretchedness, is moved with compassion. In God, therefore, mercy is nothing but the limitless love of His infinite goodness which, at the sight of the creature's miseries, stoops down to relieve and help him, to forgive and make him happy. All God's ways in dealing with us are ways of mercy. Without our wretchedness to ease, God could never have revealed the unfathomable riches of His condescending love.[49]

St. Hugh of Saint-Victor

On God as Refuge

God is become everything to you, and God has made everything for you. He has made the dwelling, and is become your refuge. This one is all, and this all is one. It is the house of God, it is the city of the King, it is the body of Christ, it is the bride of the Lamb. It is the heaven, it is the sun, it is the moon, it is the morning star, the daybreak and the evening. It is the trumpet, it is the mountain, and the desert, and the promised land. It is the ship, it is the way across the sea. It is the net, the vine, the field. It is the ark, the barn, the stable, and the manger. It is the beast of burden, and it is the horse. It is the storehouse, the court, the wedding-chamber, the tower, the camp, the battle-front. It is

---

[49] *Suffering with Christ* (Loreto Publications, 2015), 162.

the people, and the kingdom, and the priesthood. It is the flock and the shepherd, the sheep and the pastures. It is paradise, it is the garden, it is the palm, the rose, the lily. It is the fountain and the river; it is the door, it is the dove, it is the raiment, it is the pearl, it is the crown, it is the scepter, and it is the throne. It is the table and the bread, it is the spouse, the mother, the daughter and the sister.

And, to sum it all up, it was for this, with a view to this, on account of this, that the whole of Scripture was made, For this, the Word was made flesh, God was made humble, man was made sublime.

If you have this, then you have everything. If you have everything, you have nothing more to look for, and your heart is at rest.[50]

Fr. Donald Haggerty
On the Friendship of Christ

A companion who listens for a tone of voice rather than to words alone, who perceives in our eyes a communication not ready for speech, who understands a truth we want to express when it has not arrived at clarity to our confused soul—this is the nature of deeper friendship. Friendship of this nature implies a need to be known by another and, at times, the selfless attention of another. But there is another kind of friendship. The secret gaze of God upon our soul can be an exquisite form of friendship,

[50] *Noah's Ark* (Harper & Row, Publishers, 1962), 51.

incomparable to any human relations. God's friendship conveys a mysterious awareness that someone sees a truth in our soul that we do not yet recognize in ourselves. It must occasionally shock us that a secret beauty exists in us that we cannot perceive but is known to God.[51]

Thomas à Kempis

You had filled me with heavenly consolations. In You, therefore, O Lord God, I place all my hope and my refuge. On You I cast all my troubles and anguish, because whatever I have outside of You I find to be weak and unstable. It will not serve me to have many friends, nor will powerful helpers be able to assist me, nor prudent advisers to give useful answers, nor the books of learned men to console, nor any precious substance to win my freedom, nor any place, secret and beautiful though it be, to shelter me, if You Yourself do not assist, comfort, console, instruct, and guard me. For all things which seem to be for our peace and happiness are nothing when You are absent, and truly confer no happiness. You, indeed, are the fountain of all good, the height of life, the depth of all that can be spoken. To trust in You above all things is the strongest comfort of Your servants. My God, the Father of mercies, to You I look, in You I trust.[52]

---

[51] *The Contemplative Hunger* (Ignatius Press, 2016), 57.
[52] *The Imitation of Christ*, III, 59.

St. John Henry Newman

We do not know, perhaps, what or where our pain is; we are so used to it that we do not call it pain. Still it is so; we need a relief to our hearts, that they may be dark and sullen no longer, or that they may not go on feeding upon themselves. We need to escape from ourselves to something beyond; and much as we may wish it otherwise, and may try to make idols to ourselves, nothing short of God's presence is our true refuge; everything else is either a mockery, or but an expedient useful for its season or in its measure. How miserable then is he who does not practically know this great truth![53]

Blessed Columba Marmion

It is recounted of St. Mechtilde that, in her sorrows, she had the custom of taking refuge with our Lord and of abandoning herself to Him in all submission. Christ Jesus Himself had taught her to do this: "If a person wishes to make Me an acceptable offering, let him seek refuge in none beside Me in tribulation, and not complain of his griefs to anyone, but entrust to Me all the anxieties with which his heart is burdened. I will never forsake one who acts thus." We ought to accustom ourselves to tell everything to our Lord, to entrust to Him all that concerns us. "Commit thy way to the Lord," that is, reveal to Him thy thoughts, thy cares, thy anguish, and He Himself will guide thee: *Revela Domino*

---

[53] *Miscellanies, The Oxford Sermons and Other Writings* (Strahn & Co, 1870), 225.

viam tuam, et spera in eo, et ipse faciet. How do most men act? They talk over their troubles either within themselves, or to others; few go to pour out their souls at the feet of Christ Jesus. And yet that is a prayer so pleasing to God, and so fruitful a practice for the soul![54]

Fr. Robert Hugh Benson

Human friendships usually take their rise in some small external detail. We catch a phrase, we hear an inflection of a voice, we notice the look of the eyes, or a movement in walking; and the tiny experience seems to us like an initiation into a new world. We take the little event as a symbol of a universe that lies behind; we think we have detected a soul exactly suited to our own, a temperament which either from its resemblance to our own, or from a harmonious dissimilarity, is precisely fitted to be our companion. Then the process of friendship begins. . . .

Now the Divine Friendship—the consciousness, that is to say, that Christ desires our love and intimacy, and offers His own in return—usually begins in the same manner. It may be at the reception of some sacrament, such as we have received a thousand times before; or it may be as we kneel before the Crib at Christmas, or follow our Lord along the Way of the Cross. We have done these things or performed those ceremonies dutifully and lovingly again and again; yet on this sudden day a new experience comes to us. We understand, for example, for the first time that the Holy

---

[54] *Christ the Ideal of the Monk,* Part II, Chapter 16, section 14.

Child is stretching His arms from the straw, not merely to embrace the world—that would be little enough!—but to embrace our own soul in particular. We understand as we watch Jesus, bloodstained and weary, rising from His third fall, that He is asking our own very self in particular to help Him with His burden. The glance of the Divine Eyes meets our own; there passes from Him to us an emotion or a message that we had never before associated with our own relations with Him. The tiny event has happened! He has knocked at our door, and we have opened; He has called and we have answered. Henceforth, we think, He is ours and we are His. Here, at last, we tell ourselves, is the Friend for whom we have been looking so long: here is the Soul that perfectly understands our own; the one Personality which we can safely allow to dominate our own. Jesus Christ has leapt forward two thousand years, and is standing by our side; He has come down from the painting on the wall; He has risen from the straw in the manger—My Beloved is mine and I am His.[55]

St. Maria Faustina Kowalska

On one occasion, I heard these words: My daughter, tell the whole world about My inconceivable mercy. I desire that the Feast of Mercy be a refuge and shelter for all souls, and especially for poor sinners. On that day the very depths of My tender mercy are open. I

---

[55] *The Friendship of Christ* (Longmans Green and Co., 1916), 15.

pour out a whole ocean of graces upon those souls who approach the fount of My mercy. The soul that will go to Confession and receive Holy Communion shall obtain complete forgiveness of sins and punishment. On that day all the divine floodgates through which grace flow are opened. Let no soul fear to draw near to Me, even though its sins be as scarlet. My mercy is so great that no mind, be it of man or of angel, will be able to fathom it throughout all eternity. Everything that exists has come forth from the very depths of My most tender mercy. Every soul in its relation to Me will contemplate My love and mercy throughout eternity. The Feast of Mercy emerged from My very depths of tenderness. It is My desire that it be solemnly celebrated on the first Sunday after Easter. Mankind will not have peace until it turns to the Fount of My Mercy.[56]

St. Claude de la Colombiere

I glorify You in making known how good You are towards sinners, and that Your mercy prevails over all malice, that nothing can destroy it, that no matter how many times or how shamefully we fall, or how criminally, a sinner need not be driven to despair of Your pardon…It is in vain that Your enemy and mine sets new traps for me every day. He will make me lose everything else before the hope that I have in Your mercy.[57]

---

[56] *Diary, 699.*

[57] *Oeuvres de R.P. Claude de la Colombiere*, Volume VII (Avignon, 1832), Letter 89, p. 270.

St. Thérèse of Lisieux

It is not because I have been preserved from mortal sin that I go to God with confidence and love. Even if I had on my conscience all the crimes that one could commit, I am sure I would lose nothing of my confidence; I would throw myself, my heart broken with sorrow, into the arms of my Savior. I know how much He loves the prodigal son; I have heard His words to Mary Magdalene, to the woman taken in adultery, to the Samaritan woman. No, there is no one who could frighten me, for I know too well what to believe about His mercy, about His love. I know that in the twinkling of an eye, all those thousands of sins would be consumed as a drop of water cast into a blazing fire.[58]

Elder Thaddeus of Vitovnica

How will we know whether we are living according to the will of God or not? If you are sad for whatever reason, this means that you have not given yourself over to God, although from the outside it may seem that you have. He who lives according to God's will has no worries. When he needs something, he simply prays for it. If he does not receive that which he asked for, he is joyful as though he had received it. A soul that has given itself over to God has no fear of anything, not even robbers, sickness, or death. Whatever happens, such a soul always cries, 'It was the will of God.'"[59]

---

[58] *The Story of a Soul* (The Newman Press, 1955), 181.
[59] *Our Thoughts Determine Our Lives* (Platina, 2009), 7.

Fr. Jean C.J. d'Elbée

We think about examining ourselves, yet we do not think, before the examination, during the examination, and after the examination, to plunge ourselves, with all our miseries, into the consuming and transforming furnace of His Heart, which is open to us through a humble act of confidence. I am not telling you, "You believe too much in your own wretchedness." We are much more wretched than we ever realize. But I am telling you, "You do not believe enough in merciful love." We must have confidence, not in spite of our miseries, but because of them, since it is misery which attracts mercy.[60]

Blessed John of Avila

He is the Father of all mercies, whose love for His children surpasses that of all earthly parents; He alone knows the full meaning of fatherhood, and in comparison with Him, other fathers can hardly be said to love or protect their children; so that He has bidden us call no man on earth our father but Him, our only refuge.[61]

---

[60] *I Believe in Love: A Personal Retreat Based on the Teaching of St. Thérèse of Lisieux* (Sophia Institute Press, 2001).

[61] *Letter XVIII* (Stanbrook Abbey, 1904), 113.

Appendix II

A Daily Prayer

While writing Chapter 6, I was reminded how helpful prayers of renunciation have been and continue to be in my own spiritual life. These are prayers that not only offer ourselves to God and align ourselves with His will, but also explicitly reject the sins, temptations, and lies we face each day. I've found that personally and verbally renouncing these things—naming and rejecting them in prayer—can be a powerful aid to grace. I've included a very beautiful and powerful prayer from my friend John Eldredge that I know will be a source of comfort and strength to you.

Daily Prayer from John Eldredge, *Wild at Heart*

My dear Lord Jesus, I come to you now to be restored in you, renewed in you, to receive your life and your love and all the grace and mercy I so desperately need this day. I honor you as my Lord, and I surrender every aspect and dimension of my life to you. I give you my spirit, soul, and body, my heart, mind, and will. I cover myself with your blood—my spirit, soul, and body, my heart, mind, and will. I ask your Holy Spirit to restore me in you, renew me in you, and lead this time of prayer. In all that I now pray, I stand in total agreement with your Spirit and with all those praying for me by the Spirit of God and by the Spirit of God alone.

Dearest God, holy and victorious Trinity, you alone are worthy of all my worship, my heart's devotion, all my praise, all my trust, and all the glory of my life. I love you, I worship you, I give myself over to you in my heart's search for life. You alone are Life, and you have become my life. I renounce all other gods, every idol, and I give to you, God, the place in my heart and in my life that you truly deserve. This is all about you, and not about me. You are the Hero of this story, and I belong to you. I ask your forgiveness for my every sin. Search me, know me, and reveal to me where you are working in my life, and grant to me the grace of your healing and deliverance and a deep and true repentance.

Heavenly Father, thank you for loving me and choosing me before you made the world. You are my true Father—my creator, redeemer, sustainer, and the true end of all things, including my life. I love you, I trust you, I worship you. I give myself over to you, Father, to be one with you as Jesus is one with you. Thank you for proving your love for me by sending Jesus. I receive him and all his life and all his work which you ordained for me. Thank you for including me in Christ, forgiving me my sins, granting me his righteousness, making me complete in him. Thank you for making me alive with Christ, raising me with him, seating me with him at your right hand, establishing me in his authority, and anointing me with your love and your Spirit and your favor. I receive it all with thanks and give it total claim to my life—my spirit, soul, and body, my heart, mind, and will.

Jesus, thank you for coming to ransom me with your own life. I love you, worship you, trust you. I give myself over to you to be one with you in all things. I receive all the work and triumph of your cross, death, blood, and sacrifice for me, through which my every sin is atoned for, I am ransomed, delivered from the kingdom of darkness, and transferred to your kingdom; my sin nature is removed, my heart circumcised unto God, and every claim being made against me is cancelled and disarmed. I take my place now in your cross and death, dying with you to sin, to my flesh, to this world, to the evil one and his kingdom. I take up the cross and crucify my flesh with all its pride, arrogance, unbelief, and idolatry [and anything else you are currently struggling with]. I put off the old man. Apply to me all the work and triumph in your cross, death, blood, and sacrifice; I receive it with thanks and give it total claim to my spirit, soul, and body, my heart, mind, and will.

Jesus, I also receive you as my Life, and I receive all the work and triumph in your resurrection, through which you have conquered sin, death, judgment, and the evil one. Death has no power over you, nor does any foul thing. And I have been raised with you to a new life, to live your life—dead to sin and alive to God. I take my place now in your resurrection and in your life, and I give my life to you to live your life. I am saved by your life. I reign in life through your life. I receive your hope, love, faith, joy, your goodness, trueness, wisdom, power, and strength. Apply to me all the work and triumph in your resurrection; I receive it with thanks, and I give it total claim to my spirit, soul, and body, my heart, mind, and will.

Jesus, I also sincerely receive you as my authority, rule, and dominion, my everlasting victory against Satan and his kingdom, and my ability to bring your Kingdom at all times and in every way. I receive all the work and triumph in your ascension, through which Satan has been judged and cast down, and all authority in heaven and on earth has been given to you. All authority in the heavens and on this earth has been given to you, Jesus, and you are worthy to receive all glory and honor, power and dominion, now and forever. I take my place now in your authority and in your throne, through which I have been raised with you to the right hand of the Father and established in your authority. I give myself to you, to reign with you always. Apply to me all the work and triumph in your authority and your throne; I receive it with thanks and I give it total claim to my spirit, soul, and body, my heart, mind, and will.

I now bring the authority, rule, and dominion of the Lord Jesus Christ and the full work of Christ over my life today: over my home, my household, my work, over all my kingdom and domain. I bring the authority of the Lord Jesus Christ and the full work of Christ against every evil power coming against me—against every foul spirit, every foul power and device. [You might need to name them—what has been attacking you?] I cut them off in the name of the Lord; I bind and banish them from me and from my kingdom now, in the mighty name of Jesus Christ. I also bring the full work of Christ between me and every person, and I allow only the love of God and only the Spirit of God between us.

Holy Spirit, thank you for coming. I love you, I worship you, I trust you. I receive all the work and triumph in Pentecost, through which you have come, you have clothed me with power from on high, sealed me in Christ, become my union with the Father and the Son, the Spirit of truth in me, the life of God in me, my counselor, comforter, strength, and guide. I honor you as Lord, and I fully give to you every aspect and dimension of my spirit, soul, and body, my heart, mind, and will—to be filled with you, to walk in step with you in all things. Fill me afresh, Holy Spirit. Restore my union with the Father and the Son. Lead me into all truth, anoint me for all of my life and walk and calling, and lead me deeper into Jesus today. I receive you with thanks, and I give you total claim to my life.

Heavenly Father, thank you for granting to me every spiritual blessing in Christ Jesus. I claim the riches in Christ Jesus over my life today. I bring the blood of Christ once more over my spirit, soul, and body, over my heart, mind, and will. I put on the full armor of God: the belt of truth, breastplate of right-eousness, shoes of the gospel, helmet of salvation; I take up the shield of faith and sword of the Spirit, and I choose to be strong in the Lord and in the strength of your might, to pray at all times in the Spirit.

Jesus, thank you for your angels. I summon them in the name of Jesus Christ and instruct them to destroy all that is raised against me, to establish your Kingdom over me, to guard me day and night. I ask you to send forth your Spirit to raise up prayer and intercession for me. I now call forth the kingdom of God throughout my home, my house-hold, my kingdom, and domain in the authority of the Lord Jesus Christ, giving all glory and honor and thanks to him. In Jesus' name, amen.

Printed in Dunstable, United Kingdom